LET'S SAVE DEMOCRACY

First published by Aussie Trading LLC
Copyright © 2025 by Juan Rodulfo
All rights reserved.
No part of this publication may be reproduced, stored, or transmitted in any form or by any means, electronic, mechanical, photocopying, recording, scanning or otherwise without written permission from the publisher. It is illegal to copy this book, publish it on a website, or distribute it by any other means without permission.
Juan Rodulfo has no responsibility for the persistence or accuracy of URLs of external or third-party Internet websites referenced in this publication and does not warrant that the content of such websites is, or will remain, accurate or appropriate.
The names used by companies to distinguish their products are often claimed as trademarks. All trademarks and product names used in this book and on its cover, trade names, service marks, trademarks are trademarks of their respective owners. The publishers and the book are not associated with any products or suppliers mentioned in this book. None of the companies or organizations referenced in the book have endorsed it.
Library of Congress Catalog
Names: Rodulfo, Juan
ISBN: 979-8-3493-6313-9 (e-book)
ISBN: 979-8-3493-6314-6 (paperback)
ISBN: 979-8-3493-6315-3 (hardcover)
First edition
Layout by Juan Rodulfo
Cover art by Guaripete Solutions
Production: Aussie Trading, LLC
books@aussietrading.ltd
Printed in the USA

"The best way to enhance freedom in other lands, is to demonstrate that our democratic system is worthy of emulation."
President Jimmy Carter

Introduction

Today May 20, 2025, I received a text from the people that send cargo from Miami to Venezuela, informing that the custom service there, was seizing a bunch of books written by my 90 years old father, (published by me in the "free world"), because these books are an attack to the "revolution", their titles are: Torture in century 21 Socialism, The barbarities of Nicolas Maduro Dictatorship and The assassination of Captain Acosta Arévalo (Navy Officer killed by torture in the "revolution" dungeons).

I ran away from Nicolas Maduro dictatorship in 2014, to the US, because was the place where by that time was still a place where human rights were guaranteed and I knew other people who also applied for asylum, because of the same circumstances, this next October of 2025, I will reach my 11th year in US soil, if not stripped of the few "privileges[i]" I still enjoy as human and regular citizen, respectful and follower of the law.

Today I am facing again persecution, not because I politically disagree with the actual government (which is now a fact), like happened and prompted my auto exile from Venezuela, but now because of a racist and neo nazi government, can I stay silent and not warn the rest of the world about this kind of regime?

Eladio (90) and Briceida (78), my parents had 4 children, Gabriela is exiled in Canada under a UN refugee program, my brother is exiled requesting asylum here in the US, and our younger sister Katiuska was brutally assassinated back in our home country, while all of us were abroad, in a bureaucratic fight to recover at least part of our Human Privileges (Rigths), like the right to a citizenship, to vote, to travel abroad and be allowed back, etc. Luckily, our neighbors and friends have filled our empty spaces in their lives, and technology like WhatsApp and Internet keeps up together, but is a deep pain in the heart to be in this situation, caused by a minuscule group of humans, backed by small circles of power around the planet.

All these persecution stuff, once for "political" reasons, and now for "racist" reasons, all converges in a universal reason of all kind of social persecutions: been poor, they the self-nominated "powerful", hate me, and immigrants, nonwhites, Palestinians, Uygur, Rohingyas, Indigenous and even the non-wealthy-white, because they labeled us as poor, a condition created by themselves since they are the ones who accumulate the capital with no sense at all, but this is their label they tried for centuries us to believe we are, and most of the time they have succeeded, but I believe, like Dave Chapelle said in one of his specials, that we are not "poor", being "poor" is a state of mind (a dangerous one if you allow it to write your HD), we are broken, by now.

Like my father, our only weapon to defend from injustice is our pen, actually our PC, to denounce repression, corruption and crimes against humanity, to leave a path for current and future generations.

Today, May 20, 2025, the actual government of the US, is moving in a fast pace toward a neo-nazi dictatorship, enabled by a corrupt bipartisan system, a bundle of oligarchs, and a bunch of stupid people, citing Dietrich Bonhoeffer's "Theory of Stupidity". In these days most people are focused on how this people in power from the White House illegally, violently and cowardly dismantle Democracy, following their script like a cat following a red laser dot, but few in offering a viable, democratic way to get rid of these nazis forever, and rebuild the country from scratch, this is my humble point of view.

> *"The average man votes below himself; he votes with half a mind or a hundredth part of one. A man ought to vote with the whole of himself, as he worships or gets married. A man ought to vote with his head and heart, his soul and stomach, his eye for faces and his ear for music; also (when sufficiently provoked) with his hands and feet. ... The question is not so much whether only a minority of the electorate votes. The point is that only a minority of the voter votes."*
>
> **G.K. Chesterton**

Chapter 1: Referendum

Modernizing Democracy: The Case for a Next-Generation Blockchain Voting Platform

> *Democracy cannot thrive with 19th-century tools. A secure, blockchain-based voting platform would:*
>
> ✓ *Prevent foreign interference*
>
> ✓ *Boost turnout with mobile accessibility*
>
> ✓ *Restore trust via real-time audits*
>
> *The technology exists—now we need the political will to modernize.*

A Voting System for the 21st Century

The United States' voting infrastructure remains dangerously outdated. From hanging chads in 2000 to allegations of interference in 2016 and 2020, America's electoral systems are vulnerable to errors, hacking, and mistrust. To restore confidence in democracy, the U.S. must adopt a modern, blockchain-based voting platform with the following features:

1. End-to-End Encryption & Blockchain Security

2. Universal Accessibility (Mobile, Desktop, & In-Person Options)
3. Real-Time Auditing & Full Transparency
4. Scalability for Local to National Elections

This system would enhance participation, prevent fraud, and ensure verifiable results—addressing the top challenges facing elections today.

Section 1: Why Current Voting Systems Fail

1. Outdated Technology
- Many states still use paperless electronic machines with no verifiable paper trail (Brennan Center for Justice[ii], 2023).
- 15% of voting machines are over 15 years old, risking malfunctions (Verified Voting, 2022).

2. Cybersecurity Vulnerabilities
- In 2016, Russian hackers targeted election systems in all 50 states (Mueller Report, 2019).
- No federal cybersecurity standard exists for voting machines (CISA, 2023).

3. Low Accessibility
- Millions of voters face barriers due to disabilities, lack of transportation, or inflexible work hours (U.S. Election Assistance Commission[iii], 2023).

Section 2: The Blockchain Voting Solution

1. "Unhackable" & Encrypted
- Blockchain's decentralized ledger prevents tampering (Nakamoto[iv], 2008).
- Estonia's e-voting system, in use since 2005, has never been hacked (Estonian Government[v], 2023).
2. Real-Time Auditing
- Every vote is time-stamped, encrypted, and immutable, allowing instant verification (MIT Digital Currency Initiative[vi], 2022).
- No more delayed recounts—results are transparent and final.
3. Universal Accessibility
- Mobile voting for deployed troops, disabled voters, and remote workers (Voatz pilot, 2020).
- Multi-language support to assist non-native English speakers.
4. Scalability & Cost Efficiency
- Blockchain can handle millions of votes simultaneously without server crashes (IBM Security, 2021).
- Reduces costs by eliminating paper ballots and manual counting.

Section 3: Addressing Concerns

"Blockchain Isn't Perfect"

→ Solution: Hybrid systems (blockchain + paper backups) balance security and accessibility (National Academy of Sciences, 2022).

"Digital Voting Disenfranchises the Poor"

→ Solution: Free public kiosks at libraries, post offices, and community centers (U.S. Digital Response, 2023).

"What About Voter Privacy?"

→ Zero-knowledge proofs (used in Switzerland) let voters verify ballots without exposing choices (Swiss Post, 2023).

The Enduring Allure and Treacherous Path of the People's Vote: A Historian's Look at the Referendum

The referendum, that seemingly ultimate expression of democratic will where citizens directly vote on a specific proposal, stands as a fascinating and often contentious feature in the landscape of political history. As a historian, I see it not merely as a procedural tool, but as a reflection of evolving ideas about sovereignty, representation, and the very nature of governance (Gallagher & Uleri[vii], 1996). Its story is one of popular empowerment interwoven with cautionary tales of division and unintended consequences.

The roots of direct democracy, from which the referendum sprouts, can be traced to antiquity – the "ekklesia" of ancient Athens or the plebiscites of the Roman Republic offer distant echoes, though their direct lineage to modern forms is complex (Finley[viii], 1983, pp. 70-94). However, the modern referendum is largely a child of the Enlightenment and the revolutionary fervor that swept Europe and the Americas from the late 18th century. Thinkers like Jean-Jacques Rousseau, with his concept of the "general will," implicitly championed the idea that ultimate authority resides with the people, who could, and perhaps should, directly decide on fundamental matters (Rousseau[ix], 1762/1997; Pateman[x], 2003, p. 45).

Switzerland, with its long tradition of cantonal assemblies and direct citizen participation, stands as an early and enduring adopter of the referendum at a national level from the mid-19th century (Kobach[xi], 1993, pp. 30-37). For the Swiss, it became an integral part of their political DNA, used for constitutional amendments and significant legislative changes. Elsewhere, its adoption was more sporadic, often linked to moments of profound national questioning: issues of sovereignty (like Norway's secession from Sweden in 1905), territorial disposition (the Saarland referendums after World War I and II), or fundamental constitutional overhauls (Butler & Ranney[xii], 1994).

The 20th century saw the referendum employed with increasing frequency, yet its application and impact varied wildly. In some contexts, it served to legitimize new regimes or territorial changes, sometimes under conditions that cast doubt on the freedom of the vote (Suksi[xiii], 1993). In established democracies, it became a tool for resolving deeply divisive moral or social issues where parliamentary consensus was elusive – think of debates over alcohol prohibition in some nations (Blocker[xiv], 2006), or later, questions surrounding divorce, abortion, or membership in supranational bodies like the European Union (Qvortrup[xv], 2005).

Proponents have long hailed the referendum as the purest form of democracy. It offers, they argue, a clear mandate from the populace, bypassing the perceived filters and compromises of representative government (Barber[xvi], 1984). It can enhance civic engagement, educate the public on critical issues, and lend undeniable legitimacy to significant national decisions (Fishkin[xvii], 2011). When a parliament feels out of step with public sentiment, or when an issue is deemed too monumental for legislators alone, the referendum offers a direct recourse to the "owners" of sovereignty – the people[xviii][xix].

However, the historical record is replete with instances where the referendum has proven to be a double-edged sword. Critics, from the earliest days of its modern usage, have warned of its potential pitfalls:

1. Oversimplification: Complex policy questions, often requiring nuanced understanding and negotiation, can be reduced to a binary "yes/no" choice. This inevitably strips away vital detail and can lead to poorly understood outcomes (Sartori[xx], 1987, pp. 118-120).

2. The Tyranny of the Majority: A narrow victory in a referendum can impose a significant change on a deeply divided populace, potentially alienating substantial minorities and exacerbating societal fissures (Madison[xxi], 1787/1961, Federalist No. 10). The aftermath of referendums often reveals a need for reconciliation that the vote itself does not provide (LeDuc[xxii], 2003).

3. Susceptibility to Demagoguery and Misinformation: Referendum campaigns can be fertile ground for emotional appeals, populist rhetoric, and the spread of misinformation, particularly in the age of social media (Sunstein[xxiii], 2018). The intensity of a single-issue campaign can overshadow reasoned debate, with citizens potentially voting based on factors unrelated to the core question.

4. Abdication of Responsibility: Some argue that referendums allow elected representatives to sidestep difficult decisions, offloading responsibility onto an electorate that may not possess the specialized knowledge or time for thorough deliberation (Bogdanor[xxiv], 1981, pp. 150-153).

5. Rigidity: Once a decision is made by referendum, it can be politically and practically difficult to amend or reverse, even if circumstances change or negative consequences emerge (Tierney[xxv], 2012).

The wave of referendums concerning European integration – from Denmark's initial "no" to the Maastricht Treaty to the United Kingdom's 2016 vote to leave the European Union ("Brexit") – provides compelling case studies of these complexities (Glencross[xxvi], 2018). Brexit, in particular, highlighted how a single vote could unleash profound economic, social, and constitutional challenges, the full ramifications of which are still unfolding (Clarke, Goodwin, & Whiteley[xxvii], 2017). It also demonstrated the intense passions referendums can ignite and the deep societal introspection that often follows.

Looking back, the referendum is neither a panacea for democratic ills nor an inherently flawed mechanism. Its utility and wisdom are deeply contextual. Factors such as the clarity of the question, the fairness of the campaign, the level of public understanding, the provisions for implementing the result, and the broader political culture all play crucial roles in determining whether a referendum will strengthen or strain a democratic system (Morel & Qvortrup[xxviii], 2018).

As of 2025, the allure of the referendum persists, particularly in an era marked by skepticism towards traditional political institutions and a desire for more direct citizen involvement. Yet, history urges a cautious approach. It teaches us that while the people's voice is paramount, the mechanisms through which it is channeled require careful design and a profound understanding of the potential for both empowerment and peril (Hamilton[xxix], 2022). The referendum remains a powerful, sometimes unpredictable, force in the ongoing human experiment with self-governance.

The American Referendum: A Tale of Two Democracies – Federal Abstinence, State Experimentation

The referendum, a mechanism allowing citizens to vote directly on specific laws or proposals, occupies a peculiar and often misunderstood place in the American political landscape. As a historian and political analyst, I observe a fascinating dichotomy: a federal system deliberately designed without provisions for national referenda, existing alongside numerous state and local governments where direct democracy flourishes, shaping policy and igniting public debate. This bifurcated reality reflects deep historical anxieties about direct popular rule, the enduring influence of the Progressive Era, and ongoing tensions between representative and direct forms of governance in the United States.

The U.S. Constitution, drafted in 1787, established a representative republic, not a direct democracy. The Founding Fathers, while revolutionary in their assertion of popular sovereignty, were generally wary of what they termed "the turbulence and follies of democracy" (Madison[xxx], 1787/1961, Federalist No. 10). They feared that direct popular votes on legislation could lead to instability, the infringement of minority rights by impassioned majorities, and poorly crafted laws. Instead, they opted for a system of elected representatives, filtered through layers of government, to deliberate and legislate. Consequently, there is no constitutional mechanism for a national referendum or initiative in the United States (Magleby[xxxi], 1984). Proposals for such a system have surfaced periodically, particularly during times of perceived government unresponsiveness, but none have gained serious traction, reflecting a persistent elite and institutional skepticism.

However, the story of the referendum in America takes a dramatic turn at the state and local levels, primarily due to the reforms of the Progressive Era in the late 19th and early 20th centuries. Frustrated by perceived corruption, the undue influence of corporate interests (often personified by the railroad and mining trusts) on state legislatures, and the unresponsiveness of political machines, reformers championed direct democracy mechanisms as tools to empower citizens and bypass entrenched interests (Hofstadter[xxxii], 1955; Cronin[xxxiii], 1989). States like South Dakota (1898) and Oregon (1902), under the leadership of figures like William U'Ren, became pioneers, adopting the initiative, the popular referendum (allowing citizens to challenge laws passed by the legislature), and the recall (Smith & Tolbert[xxxiv], 2004).

Today, roughly half of all U.S. states, predominantly in the West and Midwest, offer some form of statewide initiative or referendum, and these tools are even more common at the municipal level (National Conference of State Legislatures [NCSL], n.d.). These mechanisms take several forms:

The Legislative Referendum: The state legislature refers to a proposed law or constitutional amendment to the voters for approval. This is the most common form and is often required for certain actions like issuing bonds or amending the state constitution.

The Popular Referendum (or "Citizens' Veto"): Citizens gather signatures to place a recently passed law on the ballot for voters to either uphold or repeal.

The Direct Initiative: Citizens draft a proposed law or constitutional amendment, gather signatures, and if successful, the measure goes directly to the ballot.

The Indirect Initiative: Citizens draft a proposal, gather signatures, and the measure is then submitted to the legislature. If the legislature does not pass it (or passes an amended version), it often then goes to the voters.

The subject matter of these state and local referenda is incredibly diverse, reflecting the pressing social, economic, and political issues of their times. Historically and contemporaneously, referenda have been used to decide:

Taxation and Spending: Perhaps most famously, California's Proposition 13 in 1978 drastically cut property taxes and limited future increases, sparking a nationwide "tax revolt" and fundamentally altering California's fiscal landscape (Sears & Citrin[xxxv], 1985). Numerous other states have seen tax limitation measures.

Social Issues: Before the Supreme Court's ruling in Obergefell v. Hodges[xxxvi] (2015) legalized same-sex marriage nationwide, numerous states held referenda on marriage definition and civil unions. More recently, states have used initiatives and referenda to address abortion access (post-Dobbs v. Jackson Women's Health Organization), marijuana legalization, and gambling (Ellis[xxxvii], 2012).

Governance and Political Reform: Term limits for elected officials, campaign finance regulations, redistricting processes, and voting rights have all been common subjects of direct democracy efforts.

Environmental and Labor Policies: Minimum wage increases, right-to-work laws, and environmental protection measures frequently appear on state ballots.

From a political analyst's perspective, the use of referenda in the U.S. presents a mixed bag of democratic outcomes. Proponents argue that they enhance citizen engagement, provide crucial checks on legislative power, allow for policy innovation that legislatures might avoid, and can break partisan gridlock (Bowler & Donovan[xxxviii], 2000). They can give voice to marginalized groups or widely held public sentiments ignored by political elites.

However, critics point to significant downsides. The high cost of qualifying and campaigning for ballot measures means that well-funded special interests can wield disproportionate influence, sometimes obscuring the "people's will" they claim to represent (Broder[xxxix], 2000). Ballot language can be complex, confusing, or even intentionally misleading, making informed decision-making difficult for voters. There's also the risk of "tyranny of the majority," where popular votes can lead to policies that disadvantage minority groups – a concern that echoes the Founding Fathers' original anxieties (Gamble[xl], 1997). Furthermore, successful initiatives can sometimes create unfunded mandates or conflict with existing laws, leading to policy incoherence and legal challenges (Persily & Anderson[xli], 2005). The rise of a "ballot measure industry" of consultants and signature-gathering firms also raises questions about the grassroots nature of some initiatives.

In conclusion, the referendum in the United States is a story of deliberate federal omission and vibrant, if sometimes chaotic, state and local experimentation. While the national government remains, a representative republic insulated from direct popular votes on policy, many states have embraced these tools as a core component of their democratic processes. The history of referenda in the U.S. reflects an ongoing negotiation between the ideals of direct citizen empowerment and the practical challenges of governing a complex, diverse society. As long as tensions persist between public sentiment and legislative action, the allure of taking issues "directly to the people" at the state and local level will undoubtedly continue, ensuring the referendum remains a dynamic and often controversial feature of American political life.

The hypothetical questions:

1.- *"Do you support the drafting and adoption of a new Constitution of the United States, replacing the current Constitution, to be developed through a constitutional convention and ratified by the people?"*

2.- *"Do you support replacing the current presidential system of government with a parliamentary system, in which the government is led by a newly legislature that includes a balanced representation of all demographics groups, elected by direct vote after eliminating electoral colleges and gerrymandering, rather than by one only person, to be implemented through a new constitution?"*

"Democracy is not an easy form of government, because it is never final; it is a living, changing organism, with a continuous shifting and adjusting of balance between individual freedom and general order."
Ilka Chase

CHAPTER 2: A NEW CONSTITUTION

The Imperative of Embedding Fundamental Human Rights in a New U.S. Constitution

The inclusion of fundamental human rights in a new U.S. constitution is essential to address historical shortcomings, respond to modern challenges, and reaffirm the nation's commitment to liberty and justice for all. As history has shown, the explicit protection of rights is not only a safeguard against tyranny but a foundation for a more equitable and just society[xlii,xliii,xliv].

The United States Constitution, since its ratification in 1789, has served as the bedrock of American democracy. While the original document established the framework of government, it was the subsequent addition of the Bill of Rights and later amendments that explicitly enshrined many fundamental human rights. As the nation contemplates the possibility of drafting a new constitution, the inclusion of comprehensive and explicit human rights protection is not only a historical necessity but also a moral imperative.

Historical Context: The Bill of Rights and Its Evolution

The original Constitution did not contain a specific enumeration of individual rights, a deficiency that nearly derailed its ratification. Responding to public outcry, the first ten amendments—collectively known as the Bill of Rights—were adopted in 1791 to guarantee essential freedoms such as speech, religion, assembly, and due process[xlv][xlvi]. These foundational rights were later expanded through amendments addressing civil rights, suffrage, and equal protection, notably with the Reconstruction Amendments following the Civil War, which abolished slavery and secured citizenship and equal rights for formerly enslaved people[xlvii][xlviii].

The Need for Explicit Human Rights Protections

1. Addressing Historical Omissions and Modern Challenges

While the Bill of Rights and subsequent amendments have provided crucial protections, gaps remain. Many rights—such as the right to privacy, health care, education, and non-discrimination based on gender or sexual orientation—are not explicitly stated in the current Constitution. As society evolves, so too must the nation's foundational legal document, ensuring that all individuals are protected from both governmental and private abuses.

2. Reinforcing Equality and Justice

The 14th Amendment's guarantee of equal protection under the law marked a significant expansion of constitutional rights, extending liberties to all citizens regardless of race. However, persistent inequalities and new forms of discrimination underscore the need for a modernized, comprehensive enumeration of rights that reflects contemporary understandings of justice and equality.

3. Meeting International Standards

Globally, modern constitutions and international treaties—such as the Universal Declaration of Human Rights—explicitly enumerate a broader array of rights, including social, economic, and cultural rights. To maintain its leadership in human rights, the United States must ensure its constitution meets or exceeds these international standards.

Recommendations for a New Constitution

A new U.S. constitution should:

- Clearly enumerate fundamental rights, including but not limited to freedom of expression, religion, assembly, privacy, education, health care, and protection from discrimination.

- Guarantee equal protection and due process for all individuals, regardless of race, gender, sexual orientation, or socioeconomic status.

- Establish robust mechanisms for the enforcement and protection of these rights, ensuring that they are not merely aspirational but legally actionable.

The actual constitution of the US was written two centuries ago, when humanity was barely discovering electricity.

According to the Pew Research Center, in an article published on May 23, 2024, Top problems facing the U.S.[xlix] are:

- Inflation
- Bipartisan work
- Healthcare
- Drug addiction
- Budget deficit
- Immigration
- Gun violence
- Violent crime
- Moral values
- Public Schools
- Climate Change
- Terrorism (both national/international)
- Infrastructure
- Racism

- Unemployment and I would add to this list: Housing, by the time the Constitution was sanctioned none of these concepts were addressed, or even known or else.

Inflation and the ability of Democrats and Republicans to work together top the public's list of the biggest problems facing the country, with 62% of Americans describing inflation as a very big problem and 60% saying this about bipartisan cooperation. Inflation, affordability of health care top Americans' list of top problems facing the country. Narrower majorities say that the affordability of healthcare (57%), drug addiction (55%) and the federal budget deficit (53%) are very big problems in the country today. And roughly half say that illegal immigration (51%), gun violence (49%), violent crime (48%) and the state of moral values (46%) are each very big problems. The quality of public K-12 schools, climate change and international terrorism are lower on the public's list of the country's top problems, though majorities rate these and several other issues included in the survey as at least moderately big problems.

So, there is a huge gap between what was planned and what is really happening today, with barely any constitutional or legal boundaries to be prevented, contained or punished, this is another reason why this country needs a new constitution.

But a constitution written by the representatives of the people, elected in a balanced, fair and clear electoral process. Once the Referendum to decide whether to rebuild the state from scratch has positive results, this new constitution should be approved by the same electoral process of National Referendum.

Constitutionalizing Fundamental Rights: A Framework for Addressing America's Greatest Challenges

The U.S. must evolve beyond 18th-century rights frameworks. Constitutionalizing these guarantees would address systemic inequities and align America with global standards of human dignity.

The United States faces systemic crises—economic inequality, declining public health, educational disparities, housing insecurity, and environmental threats—that demand structural solutions. While the Constitution guarantees civil and political rights, it does not explicitly protect economic and social rights, leaving citizens vulnerable to market fluctuations and political whims. By constitutionally enshrining healthcare, education (including higher education), universal basic income (UBI), inflation-indexed wages, housing, abortion access, clean water, postal services, and internet access, the U.S. could address its most pressing problems while ensuring long-term stability and equity.

The Case for Constitutionalizing Economic and Social Rights

1. Healthcare as a Right

Problem: The U.S. spends more on healthcare than any developed nation yet has worse outcomes, with 30 million uninsured (KFF[l], 2023).
Solution: Following models like Germany's constitutional healthcare guarantee (Art. 74) would reduce costs and improve access (WHO[li], 2020).
Precedent: The Affordable Care Act (2010) was a step forward but remains vulnerable to repeal (Obamacare Cases, 2012-2021).

2. Education Through University Level

Problem: Student debt exceeds $1.7 trillion, pricing many out of higher education (Federal Reserve[lii], 2023).
Solution: Countries like Finland guarantee tuition-free university in their

constitutions (Ministry of Education and Culture, 2021).

U.S. Precedent: Brown v. Board of Education (1954) affirmed education's importance but stopped short of declaring it a right.

3. Universal Basic Income (UBI)

Problem: Automation and gig work destabilize incomes, with 40% of Americans unable to cover a $400 emergency (Federal Reserve, 2022).

Solution: Pilot programs (e.g., Stockton, CA) show UBI reduces poverty without reducing the work ethic (Stanford Basic Income Lab[liii], 2021).

Constitutional Model: Brazil's 1988 Constitution includes social welfare rights (Art. 6).

4. Wages Indexed Above Inflation

Problem: Stagnant wages since the 1970s erode purchasing power (EPI[liv], 2023).

Solution: Tying minimum wage to inflation + productivity (as in Australia) ensures fair compensation (OECD[lv], 2022).

5. Housing as a Right

Problem: 580,000+ Americans are homeless, while investors buy up affordable housing (HUD, 2023).

Solution: South Africa's constitution (Art. 26) mandates progressive housing access (Tissington, 2011).

6. Abortion Access

Problem: Dobbs v. Jackson (2022) revoked federal protections, creating a patchwork of bans.

Solution: Constitutionalizing abortion rights (like Ireland's 2018 repeal of the 8th Amendment) ensures bodily autonomy (Center for Reproductive Rights[lvi], 2023).

7. Clean Water

Problem: Flint, MI, and Jackson, MS, crises prove U.S. water infrastructure is failing.

Solution: The UN recognizes water as a human right; South Africa's constitution (Sec. 27) enforces this (UN Resolution 64/292[lvii], 2010).

8. Postal Service Guarantee

Problem: Privatization threats endanger rural and low-income access.
Solution: France's constitution protects postal services as a public good (Art. 34).

9. Internet Access

Problem: The digital divide exacerbates inequality (42 million lack broadband, FCC 2023).
Solution: Estonia's constitution treats internet access as a utility (e-Estonia, 2022).

Why Constitutionalizing is Necessary

- Prevents Rollbacks: Legislation (e.g., ACA, Roe) can be overturned; constitutional rights are more durable.
- Reduces Inequality: Market-based solutions fail marginalized groups.
- Aligns with Global Norms: 75% of constitutions protect at least one social right (UN Development Programme, 2020).

Implementation Pathways
1. A new Constitution

Reimagining Immigration as an Engine of American Prosperity: A Case for Reform

The U.S. must transition from a punitive to a proactive immigration system—one that treats newcomers as nation-builders. By offering citizenship after 5 years, voting rights for taxpayers, and working visas with dignity, America can secure its future as the world's leading economy.

A Pro-Growth Immigration Vision

The United States has always been a nation of immigrants—a fact central to its economic strength, cultural dynamism, and global competitiveness. Yet, despite immigrants contributing $2 trillion annually to U.S. GDP (New American Economy[lviii], 2022), the current immigration system treats them as a security threat rather than a national asset. To maximize America's potential, the immigration system must shift from policing and persecution to integration and opportunity.

Key reforms should include:

1. A pathway to citizenship for undocumented immigrants with 5+ years of residence and no criminal record

2. Work visas with labor protections and a path to voting rights after 5 years

3. Streamlined legal immigration to address labor shortages

This approach aligns with America's historical reliance on immigrant labor while fostering long-term economic growth.

Section 1: Immigrants Strengthen the U.S. Economy

Job Creation & Entrepreneurship

- Immigrants are 80% more likely to start businesses than native-born Americans (Harvard Business Review, 2022).

- 45% of Fortune 500 companies were founded by immigrants or their children (Center for American Entrepreneurship, 2023).

Labor Force Vitality

- Immigrants fill critical gaps in healthcare, agriculture, and STEM fields (Bureau of Labor Statistics, 2023).

- Without immigrants, the U.S. would face a shortage of 6.5 million workers by 2035 (Pew Research Center[lix], 2023).

Tax Contributions

- Undocumented immigrants alone pay $11.7 billion in state/local taxes annually (Institute on Taxation and Economic Policy, 2023).

Section 2: The Case for a 5-Year Pathway to Citizenship

Why 5 Years?
- Historical Precedent: The U.S. once had no numerical limits on immigration and allowed faster naturalization (U.S. Citizenship and Immigration Services, 2021).
- Social Integration: Studies show immigrants who stay 5+ years have deep community ties (National Academies of Sciences[lx], 2022).

Proposed Policy:
- Undocumented immigrants with 5+ years of residence, no felonies, and steady employment gain permanent residency.
- Work visa holders (H-1B, seasonal workers) earn voting rights after 5 years, ensuring political representation.

Section 3: Work Visas with Voting Rights—A Democratic Imperative

The Problem:
- 11 million non-citizen workers' pay taxes but have no voting power (Migration Policy Institute, 2023).
- Local economies depend on immigrants, yet they lack a political voice (American Immigration Council[lxi], 2023).

The Solution:

- Extend municipal/state voting rights to long-term visa holders (as in Maryland and Vermont).
- Federal voting rights after 5 years of tax contributions.

Section 4: Upgrading Immigration from Policing to Workforce Development

End Mass Deportations
- ICE deportations cost $8 billion/year but don't reduce undocumented migration (Cato Institute[lxii], 2023).

Replace Detention with Integration Programs
- Canada's model of community sponsorship cuts costs and boosts success rates (World Bank, 2023).

Fast-Track High-Demand Skills
- Green cards for STEM graduates, as proposed in the 2023 DHS rule changes.

Counterarguments & Rebuttals

"Immigrants take jobs."
→ False. Immigrants expand job markets—for every 100 new immigrants, 86 jobs are created (National Bureau of Economic Research, 2023).

"Voting is for citizens only."

→ Historical exception: The U.S. allowed non-citizen voting in 22 states pre-1920 (Raskin[lxiii], 2023).

"Amnesty rewards lawbreaking."
→ Reality: Most undocumented immigrants overstay visas (DHS, 2023)—a civil, not criminal, issue.

Ending America's Gun Violence Pandemic: A Policy Framework for Radical Reform

A Safer America is Possible

The U.S. does not have to live with gun violence. By banning weapons of war, demilitarizing police, screening gun owners, and tracking firearms, America can follow Australia, the UK, and Japan in drastically reducing deaths. The Constitution allows for public safety—now we need the political will to act.

The United States faces a gun violence pandemic, with over 45,000 firearm deaths annually (CDC[lxiv], 2022), surpassing casualties from many modern wars. Mass shootings, police killings, and armed domestic disputes have normalized gun violence as an American epidemic. Yet, despite public outrage, legislative inaction persists due to political gridlock and the gun lobby's influence. To meaningfully

reduce gun deaths, the U.S. must adopt four key constitutional reforms:
1. Banning military-grade weapons for civilians
2. Restricting police from routinely carrying firearms (only authorized in pre-approved high-risk operations)
3. Mandating psychological, criminal, and behavioral evaluations for gun owners
4. Implementing a national firearm registry with strict oversight

These measures align with successful policies in peer nations and historical U.S. precedents for regulating dangerous weapons.

1. Banning War Weapons in Civilian Hands

The Problem
- AR-15s and similar semi-automatic rifles—designed for warfare—are frequently used in mass shootings (e.g., Uvalde, Sandy Hook, Parkland) (FBI[lxv], 2023).
- The 1994 Federal Assault Weapons Ban reduced mass shootings but expired in 2004; killings surged afterward (Webster et al.[lxvi], 2014).

The Solution
- Reinstate and expand the assault weapons ban to include high-capacity magazines and modifications (e.g., bump stocks).

- Buyback programs, as seen in Australia (1996), reduced gun deaths by 50%+ (Harvard Injury Control Research Center[lxvii], 2016).

2. Disarming Routine Policing

The Problem
- U.S. police kill ~1,000 people annually—disproportionately Black and Latino individuals (Mapping Police Violence, 2023).
- Many European countries (UK, Norway, Iceland) largely unarm beat cops; deadly force is rare (Policing Insight, 2021).

The Solution
- Only allow firearms in pre-approved high-risk operations (e.g., armed standoffs).
- Expand non-lethal alternatives (e.g., tasers, crisis de-escalation teams).

3. Psychological & Criminal Screening for Gun Owners

The Problem
- 80% of mass shooters exhibited warning signs before killing (NYPD[lxviii], 2018).
- Domestic abusers are 5x more likely to murder partners if they own guns (Everytown Research[lxix], 2022).

The Solution
- Mandatory mental health & background checks (including social media monitoring).

- "Red flag" laws to temporarily disarm high-risk individuals (RAND[lxx], 2020).

4. A National Firearm Registry

The Problem
- 30% of guns used in crimes are obtained illegally due to weak tracking (ATF, 2021).
- The U.S. has no federal gun registry, unlike cars or prescription drugs.
The Solution
- Universal registration with serial numbers tied to owners.
- Strict penalties for unregistered sales.

Counterarguments & Rebuttals

- "Guns don't kill people, people do."
→ But access to guns turns conflicts lethal. The U.S. has 5x the homicide rate of disarmed nations (Small Arms Survey, 2018).
- "The Second Amendment forbids restrictions."
→ Heller (2008) allowed "reasonable regulations" (Scalia's opinion). Even conservative justices support bans on "dangerous and unusual weapons."
- "Police need guns for safety."
→ UK police face fewer deaths than U.S. cops despite being unarmed (OECD, 2022).

Restoring Moral Values in Governance and Society: A Blueprint for Ethical Reform

Moral decay is not inevitable—it's a policy choice. By "contractualizing" political integrity, valuing educators, and supporting families, the U.S. can revive the ethical foundations of democracy.

A Moral Renaissance Through Policy

The erosion of moral values in public life—evidenced by political corruption, underpaid educators, and inadequate family protection, demands structural reforms. To rebuild trust and integrity, the U.S. must:

1. Replace ceremonial oaths for politicians with legally binding performance contracts
2. Raise teacher salaries to reflect their societal importance
3. Strengthen family protections (paid parental leave, breastfeeding rights, childcare support)

These measures would realign institutions with the moral foundations of accountability, dignity, and equity.

Section 1: Replacing Political Oaths with Enforceable Contracts

The Problem with Symbolic Oaths
- Oaths of office (e.g., on Bibles) are unenforceable rituals. Over 100 federal officials have been convicted of corruption since 2000 (DOJ[lxxi], 2023).
- No legal recourse exists for politicians who violate sworn duties (CRS, 2022).

The Solution: Performance-Based Contracts
- Key provisions:
- Financial penalties for unmet campaign promises (e.g., Singapore's parliamentary accountability model).
- Mandatory restitution for corruption (as in Norway's public service laws).
- Precedent: Corporate executives face claw back clauses; politicians should too (Harvard Law Review, 2021).

Section 2: Elevating Teachers as Moral Architects

The Current Crisis
- Teachers earn 23% less than similarly educated professionals (EPI[lxxii], 2023).
- 55% of educators work second jobs (NEA, 2022), undermining morale and student outcomes.

Policy Reforms
- Federal minimum teacher salary of $75,000 (benchmarked to engineers' wages).
- Tax credits for school supplies (expanding the Educator Expense Deduction).
- Student loan forgiveness for 10 years of service (as in the TEACH Grant Program).

Moral Impact: Societies that value educators see higher civic engagement (OECD[lxxiii], 2022).

Section 3: Protecting Families to Strengthen Societal Values

The U.S. Lag in Family Policy
- No federal paid parental leave (only 12 weeks unpaid via FMLA).
- The U.S. ranks last among OECD nations for breastfeeding support (WHO[lxxiv], 2023).

Proposed Reforms

1. 12-Month Paid Parental Leave
   - Funded via payroll taxes (modeled on Sweden's 480-day policy).
   - Equal leave for fathers to reduce gender inequity (UN Women, 2022).

2. Breastfeeding Protections
   - Mandated lactation spaces in all workplaces (expanding the PUMP Act).
   - Tax incentives for employers with on-site childcare.

3. Childcare Subsidies
 - Cap costs at 7% of income (as in Biden's 2023 Executive Order).

Counterarguments & Rebuttals

"Contracts would deter public service."
→ Data: Countries with strict accountability (e.g., Denmark) have higher trust in government (Transparency International, 2023).
"Teacher raises are too expensive."
→ ROI: Every $1 invested in teacher pay yields $1.30 in economic growth (Brookings, 2022).
"Parental leave hurts businesses."
→ Evidence: Companies with paid leave report 25% lower turnover (Harvard Business School, 2021).

Direct Demographic Representation in a U.S. Congress with no Senate

The vision of national legislature that perfectly reflects the demographic tapestry of its citizenry is a potent one, often invoked in discussions about political equality and representation. This article explores a hypothetical electoral system for the United States Congress designed to achieve such an outcome: electing a body of representatives through direct vote, with seats allocated to ensure proportional representation based on major demographic groups (excluding religion), as defined by the most recent U.S. Census. I will examine the theoretical appeal of such a system, its potential benefits, and the profound constitutional, practical, and philosophical challenges it would inevitably encounter.

The American Ideal of Representation: A Contested History

The current U.S. system for electing members of Congress is primarily based on geographic representation through single-member districts, decided by first-past-the-post voting (winner-take-all). While the principle of "one person, one vote" is central, the system does not inherently guarantee, nor was it primarily designed for, descriptive representation—where the legislature mirrors the demographic characteristics of the population (Pitkin[lxxv], 1967). The writers of the constitution, while establishing a republic rooted in popular sovereignty, were more focused on representation of states (in the Senate) and populations within geographic areas (in the House), mediated by elected representatives rather than direct demographic mirroring (Madison, Hamilton, & Jay[lxxvi], 1788/1961).

Throughout American history, debates over who is represented and how have been continuous. From the three-fifths compromise to the struggles for women's suffrage, African American voting rights (culminating in the Voting Rights Act of 1965), and ongoing debates about gerrymandering and minority-majority districts, the quest for fairer representation has been a recurring theme (Keyssar[lxxvii], 2000; Davidson & Grofman[lxxviii], 1994). The proposed system of direct demographic representation takes this quest to a fundamentally different level.

Design for Demographic Parity: The Mechanics of a Hypothetical System

Implementing such a system would require a radical overhaul of American electoral machinery. Key considerations would include:

Defining Demographic Groups: The U.S. Census Bureau already collects extensive data on race, ethnicity, age, sex, and other characteristics (U.S. Census Bureau, n.d.). For this system, "main demographic groups" would need to be officially defined and their proportions in the population established. This process itself would be politically charged. For instance, how would intersecting identities (e.g., an individual identifying with multiple racial or ethnic groups) be handled for seat allocation? The exclusion of religion simplifies one dimension but leaves many complex categories.

Seat Allocation: The 435 seats in the House of Representatives (and potentially Senate seats, though this raises further constitutional issues regarding state representation) would be allocated proportionally to these defined demographic groups. For example, if a particular ethnic group constitutes 15% of the U.S. population according to the latest census, they would be entitled to approximately 65 seats in the House. Thus, Congress and Senate must be expanded in order to allocate as many representatives as needed.

Voting Mechanism: A "direct vote" could take several forms:

National Party Lists with Demographic Quotas: Voters could cast ballots for political parties, and parties would be required to fill their allocated share of seats with candidates meeting specific demographic profiles to achieve overall congressional proportionality.

Separate Demographic Electorates: Voters might be asked to identify with a primary demographic group and vote for candidates running to represent that specific group. This approach, however, raises significant concerns about social division and individual identity.

Mixed Systems: Combinations of geographic and demographic representation could be envisioned, though this would dilute the "direct demographic" principle.

Potential Advantages: The Allure of a Reflective Legislature

Proponents of such a system might argue about several benefits:

Enhanced Descriptive Representation: The most obvious outcome would be a Congress that visually and experientially "looks like" America, potentially increasing feelings of inclusion and legitimacy among historically underrepresented groups (Mansbridge[lxxix], 1999).

Diverse Perspectives in Policymaking: Representatives from various demographic backgrounds could bring a wider range of lived experiences and perspectives to policy debates, potentially leading to more nuanced and responsive legislation.

Increased Political Engagement: Seeing "people like them" in positions of power might encourage greater political interest and participation from members of various demographic communities.

Addressing Systemic Underrepresentation: The system would directly address the persistent underrepresentation of certain groups that current electoral mechanisms have failed to fully rectify.

Profound Challenges and Criticisms

Despite its theoretical appeal to some, a system of direct demographic representation would face monumental obstacles:

Constitutional Revolution: Implementing this system would necessitate fundamental amendments to the U.S. Constitution. Article I, which outlines congressional representation based on states and population counts within them, would require complete rewriting. The Equal Protection Clause of the Fourteenth Amendment could be interpreted in conflicting ways—either supporting such a system as a remedy for past underrepresentation or opposing it as a form of group-based allocation that infringes on individual rights to equal treatment regardless of demographic affiliation (Regents of the Univ. of California v. Bakke[lxxx], 1978). This is a reason why it is needed a new constitution from scratch.

The Perils of Defining and Entrenching Groups: The act of the state officially categorizing its citizens into demographic blocks for electoral purposes is fraught with historical dangers. It risks essentializing complex individual identities, reducing individuals to single demographic markers, and potentially fostering social and political division rather than unity (Appiah[lxxxi], 2018). Who decides the "main" groups? What about new or evolving identities?

Impact on Voter Choice and Political Parties: Would voters be encouraged to vote primarily along demographic lines, potentially overshadowing policy preferences or broader ideological alignments? The role and nature of political parties would be drastically altered. Would parties become mere aggregators of demographic quotas, or would they fracture along these lines?

Tokenism vs. Substantive Representation: There's a risk that representatives elected under such a system might be viewed as "tokens" of their group rather than legislators accountable to a broader constituency or national interest. Descriptive representation does not automatically guarantee substantive representation (acting for the interests of a group) (Pitkin, 1967).

Practical Implementation Nightmare: The logistical complexity of managing such a system—from voter registration based on demographic identity (if required) to ensure accurate allocation and preventing manipulation—would be immense.

How would candidates be nominated and vetted for demographic authenticity?

Individual Rights vs. Group Rights: The system prioritizes group representation, which could conflict with the strong emphasis on individual rights within American political thought. Can an individual effectively be represented if their primary identity doesn't align with the pre-defined group they are categorized into?

National Unity and Common Good: A legislature explicitly structured around demographic divisions might struggle to foster a sense of national unity or prioritize a common good that transcends group interests. It could lead to politics of inter-group competition for resources and influence.

Historical and Comparative Insights

While no major democracy has implemented a system as comprehensively based on demographic proportionality as the one described, some countries utilize quotas for specific groups (e.g., gender quotas in party lists, reserved seats for ethnic minorities in some legislatures) (Krook[lxxxii], 2009). These are typically integrated within existing electoral frameworks (like proportional representation party-list systems or even single-member districts) rather than forming the entire basis of representation. Experiences with consociationalism systems, which allocate power among distinct religious or linguistic groups (e.g., Lebanon, historically Belgium), offer cautionary tales about entrenching group identities in the political structure, though these often include religious categories explicitly excluded in this proposal (Lijphart[lxxxiii], 1977).

The U.S. own experience with creating "majority-minority" districts under the Voting Rights Act to enhance minority representation, while far less radical, has been contentious, facing legal challenges and debates about whether it effectively serves minority interests or leads to further segregation (Guinier[lxxxiv], 1994).

A Radical Vision with Deep Dilemmas

The concept of electing a U.S. Congress based on direct demographic representation is a radical departure from American political tradition and constitutional design. While it holds the allure of creating a legislature that is a "mirror of the nation" and potentially addressing persistent underrepresentation, it also presents profound challenges. The process of officially categorizing citizens, the potential for social division, the impact on individual voter choice and political parties, and the immense constitutional hurdles make its implementation highly problematic.

Ultimately, such a proposal forces a confrontation with fundamental questions about the nature of representation: Is the primary goal to reflect the nation's demographic makeup, or to facilitate the representation of diverse interests and ideologies through a system of accountable representatives chosen by geographically defined electorates? While striving for a more inclusive and representative democracy is a laudable goal, the path of direct demographic apportionment, as history and political analysis suggest, is fraught with complexities that could undermine other core democratic values.

Toward a More Representative Democracy

The Electoral College and gerrymandering distort political representation, entrench partisan power, and diminish voter confidence. Getting rid off these systems is crucial for ensuring that every vote carries equal weight and that elected officials truly reflect the will of the people. While eliminating these structures faces political resistance, the long-term health of American democracy depends on it.

The Case for Eliminating the Electoral College and Gerrymandering in U.S. Elections

The United States prides itself on being a beacon of democracy, yet its electoral system contains two deeply flawed mechanisms that distort political representation: the Electoral College and gerrymandering. Both institutions undermine the principle of "one person, one vote," disproportionately favoring certain groups over others and weakening democratic legitimacy. Reforming or abolishing these systems is essential to ensuring fair and equitable elections.

The Electoral College: An Outdated and Undemocratic System

The Electoral College, established by the constitution writers as a compromise between congressional and popular election of the president, no longer serves its original purpose. Instead, it creates significant disparities in voter influence based on geography.

Key Problems with the Electoral College

1. Disproportionate Influence of Swing States
    - Presidential campaigns focus overwhelmingly on a handful of battleground states (e.g., Florida, Pennsylvania, Michigan),

while voters in non-competitive states (e.g., California, Texas) are largely ignored (Edwards[lxxxv], 2019).
- This leads to unequal political attention and policy prioritization, skewing national agendas toward swing-state interests.

2. The Risk of the Winner Losing the Popular Vote
- Five U.S. presidents—including Donald Trump (2016) and George W. Bush (2000)—have won the Electoral College while losing the national popular vote (National Archives[lxxxvi], 2021).
- This undermines the democratic principle that the candidate with the most votes should win.

3. Discouragement of Voter Turnout in Non-Competitive States
- Voters in solidly "red" or "blue" states often feel their votes do not matter, leading to lower participation (Bugh[lxxxvii], 2016).

Potential Solutions
- National Popular Vote Interstate Compact (NPVIC): States agreeing to award their electoral votes to the national popular vote winner (Koza et al.[lxxxviii], 2013).
- Constitutional Amendment: Abolishing the Electoral College entirely, though this faces significant political hurdles.

Gerrymandering: Manipulating Democracy Through Redistricting

Gerrymandering—the deliberate drawing of electoral districts to favor one political party—further erodes fair representation. Both Democrats and Republicans engage in this practice, but its consequences harm democratic accountability.

Key Problems with Gerrymandering

1. Partisan Bias in Elections

 - Legislators choose their voters rather than voters choosing their representatives, leading to uncompetitive districts (McGann et al.[lxxxix], 2016).

 - In 2012, Republicans won 33 more House seats than expected based on their vote share due to gerrymandering (Wang[xc], 2016).

2. Racial and Minority Vote Dilution

 - Gerrymandering has been used to weaken minority voting power, violating the Voting Rights Act (VRA) of 1965 (Li & Grofman[xci], 2020).

3. Polarization and Gridlock

 - Safe districts incentivize extreme partisanship, as politicians cater only to their base rather than seeking bipartisan compromise (Drutman[xcii], 2020).

Potential Solutions

- Independent Redistricting Commissions: States like California and Arizona use nonpartisan panels to draw fairer districts (Cirincione & Darling[xciii], 2019).
- Algorithmic Redistricting: Computer-generated maps based on neutral criteria (e.g., compactness, community integrity) (Stephanopoulos & McGhee[xciv], 2015).
- Strengthening the Voting Rights Act: Restoring federal oversight of redistricting in states with a history of discrimination (Brennan Center for Justice, 2022).
- No gerrymandering

The Imperative of Church State Separation: Reexamining Religious Symbols in Government Functions

The constitutional principle of separation of church and state, rooted in the First Amendment's Establishment Clause, remains one of the most critical safeguards of religious freedom and democratic equality in the United States. However, despite this foundational doctrine, numerous governmental practices—such as the inclusion of "In God We Trust" on currency, the use of the Christian Bible in oaths of office, and the display of religious symbols in public buildings—blur the line between religion and state. These traditions, though often defended as historical or ceremonial, undermine the neutrality required of a secular government and risk marginalizing no Christian and nonreligious citizens. This article examines why strict adherence to church state separation necessitates reevaluating these practices.

Historical and Constitutional Foundations

The framers of the Constitution, influenced by Enlightenment ideals and the dangers of state-imposed religion, deliberately crafted a secular government. Key historical and legal precedents include:

The First Amendment (1791): Prohibits Congress from establishing a religion or interfering with free exercise (Cornell Law School[xcv], n.d.).

Thomas Jefferson's "Wall of Separation" (1802): Reinforced the idea that government must remain neutral in religious matters (Jefferson[xcvi], 1802).

Everson v. Board of Education (1947): Applied the Establishment Clause to state governments, mandating nationwide church state separation (Everson v. Board of Education, 1947).

Despite these principles, religious symbolism persists in government functions, raising constitutional and ethical concerns.

Key Issues Undermining Church State Separation

1. "In God We Trust" on Currency

Origins: Added during the Cold War (1956) as a counter to "godless communism," not as a founding era tradition (Green[xcvii], 2015).

Constitutional Concerns:

Violates neutrality by endorsing monotheistic belief (Aronow v. United States[xcviii], 1970).

Marginalizes atheists, polytheists, and nontheistic citizens (American Humanist Association v. United States[xcix], 2016).

Proposed Solution: Redesign currency to reflect national unity without religious language (e.g., "E Pluribus Unum") (Kramnick & Moore[c], 2005).

2. Swearing Oaths on the Christian Bible

Historical Context: Common but never constitutionally required; many founders (e.g., John Quincy Adams) used law books instead (Lambert[ci], 2003).

Legal Precedents:

Torcaso v. Watkins (1961): Banned religious tests for public office.

Alternatives (affirmations) exist but are often stigmatized (Pfeffer, 1967).

Equity Issue: Non-Christian officials (e.g., Muslims, Hindus, secularists) face implicit pressure to conform (Seidel[cii], 2019).

3. Religious Displays in Public Buildings

Ten Commandments Monuments:

McCreary County v. ACLU (2005): Ruled unconstitutional when displaying an overtly religious purpose.

Van Orden v. Perry (2005): Allowed only if part of a broader historical exhibit (Lupu & Tuttle, 2009).

Nativity Scenes & Crosses:

Lynch v. Donnelly (1984): Permitted only if part of a secular holiday display.

American Legion v. American Humanist Association (2019): Upheld a war memorial cross, but dissent warned of Christian favoritism (Laycock[ciii], 2020).

Why Strict Separation Matters

1. **Religious Pluralism**: The U.S. is increasingly diverse—25% unaffiliated, with growing Hindu, Muslim, and secular populations (Pew Research Center[civ], 2022). Government neutrality ensures inclusivity.
2. **Preventing Coercion**: Even symbolic endorsements can alienate minority groups (e.g., atheist veterans opposed to cross

memorials) (American Humanist Association, 2019).

3. **Global Precedent**: Secular democracies (e.g., France, India) avoid state sponsored religious symbols to prevent sectarian conflict (Bhargava[cv], 2013).

Reforms for a Religiously Neutral Government

1. **Currency**: Replace "In God We Trust" with secular mottos (e.g., "Liberty," "E Pluribus Unum").
2. **Oaths of Office**: Normalize secular affirmations and discourage Bible use.
3. **Public Displays**: Remove standalone religious symbols; permit only in historical contexts.

The separation of church and state is not an attack on religion but a protection for all beliefs. By removing religious language from currency, secularizing oaths, and limiting religious displays, the U.S. can uphold its constitutional promise of equality. As Justice Sandra Day O'Connor warned, government endorsements of

> *religion send "a message to nonadherent that they are outsiders" (Lynch v. Donnelly, 1984, concurrence). A truly pluralistic democracy demands nothing less than strict neutrality.*

The Crisis of Purpose in American Education

> *The Founders understood education as democracy's safeguard - Jefferson called it "the only sure foundation of liberty." By constitutionally guaranteeing education and recentering curricula on citizenship, we can produce both thoughtful voters and innovative professionals. Our survival as a democratic nation depends on this dual transformation.*

Education for a Functioning Democracy

The United States education system stands at a crossroads. Designed in the industrial era to produce compliant workers, our schools now fail to meet the needs of a 21st-century democracy. With only 24% of high school graduates demonstrating civic competency (NAEP[cvi], 2022) and employers reporting that 58% of graduates lack critical thinking skills (Business Roundtable[cvii], 2023), we must fundamentally reorient education around two pillars:

1. Constitutional guarantee of education from pre-K through university
2. Curriculum focused first on developing engaged citizens, then career-ready professionals

This dual transformation would address America's crisis of democratic participation while maintaining economic competitiveness.

Section I: Why Education Must Become a Constitutional Right

The Current Inequity
- 1.2 million students drop out annually due to financial pressures (NCES, 2023)
- Only 28% of low-income students complete college vs. 68% of high-income peers (Postsecondary National Policy Institute, 2023)

International Models
- Germany's Basic Law (Article 7) guarantees tuition-free university
- Finland's constitutional education right yields 93% graduation rates (OECD[cviii], 2023)

Proposed Amendment Language
"Congress shall establish and maintain a system of free public education from early childhood through postsecondary study, ensuring equal opportunity for all citizens to develop the knowledge and skills necessary for

democratic participation and economic productivity."

Section 2: The Citizen-First Curriculum Model

Elementary School: Foundations of Democratic Thinking
- Replace rote memorization with:
  - Philosophy for Children programs developing questioning skills (Lipman[cix], 2003)
  - Local government simulations starting in 3rd grade
  - Media literacy integrated across subjects (Stanford History Education Group[cx], 2021)

Middle School: Systems Thinking in Action
- Mandatory courses in:
  - Comparative political systems
  - Scientific skepticism and epistemology
  - Community-based problem-solving projects

High School: Applied Democratic Practice
- Replace electives with:
  - Legislative internships (local/state government)
  - Debate and rhetorical requirements
  - "Democracy Lab" capstone projects solving real community issues

University: Specialization with Civic Anchors
- All majors require:
  - 2 semesters of deliberative democracy seminars
  - Public policy analysis in discipline context
  - 400-hour community engagement component

Section 3: Implementation Framework

Constitutional Pathway
- State-level education amendments (following NY's 2022 "Right to Education" proposal)
- Federal funding tied to curriculum standards (updating ESEA)

Teacher Revolution
- Triple compensation for social studies educators
- National Teacher Corps specializing in democratic pedagogy

Assessment Reform
- Replace standardized tests with:
  - Civic engagement portfolios
  - Deliberative forums evaluation
  - Community impact measurements

Counterarguments and Rebuttals
"This would be too expensive"

→ Every $1 invested in early civic education yields $13 in long-term societal benefits (Levine[cxi], 2022)

"Schools shouldn't be political"
→ Teaching democratic skills isn't partisan - Switzerland's non-ideological civic education produces 87% voter turnout (IDEA, 2023)

"We need job training first"
→ Countries with citizen-focused education (Finland, Canada) actually score higher on workforce readiness indices (WEF[cxii], 2023)

Climate Readiness: A Historical Imperative for National Survival

Societies that heed environmental warnings—like the Dutch adapting to sea rise—thrive. Those that don't—like Easter Island—collapse. The U.S. must act now to avoid a climate dystopia and build a resilient future.

Choosing the Right Side of History

The Lessons of History and the Urgency of Now.

History shows that civilizations thrive when they adapt to environmental challenges and collapse when they ignore them. From the Mayan droughts to Dust Bowl migrations, societies that fail to prepare for ecological shifts face catastrophic consequences (Diamond[cxiii], 2005). Today, the U.S. confronts a climate emergency—rising seas, intensifying wildfires, and extreme weather threaten infrastructure, agriculture, and national security. To avoid historical mistakes, America must adopt proactive, science-based climate adaptation policies that:

1. Modernize infrastructure to withstand extreme weather
2. Transition to renewable energy while protecting vulnerable workers
3. Establish a National Climate Resilience Corps for disaster response
4. Enact legal safeguards to prevent climate-driven displacement

The window of action is closing—but history also shows that well-prepared nations endure.

Section 1: Climate Change as a Threat Multiplier

1. Infrastructure Vulnerabilities
- $150 billion in annual climate-related disaster damages (NOAA[cxiv], 2023)
- 60% of U.S. roads are in poor condition, worsening flood risks (ASCE, 2023)

Solution:
- Climate-proof construction codes (e.g., elevating buildings in flood zones)

- Grid modernization to prevent blackouts (like Texas' 2021 freeze)
   2. National Security Risks
   - Pentagon reports climate change intensifies conflicts (DoD[cxv], 2023)
   - Climate migration could displace 13 million Americans by 2100 (PNAS, 2022)
   Solution:
   - Military climate readiness programs (e.g., fortifying bases against sea rise)
   - Legal protections for climate refugees

Section 2: A Just Transition to Renewable Energy

   1. Phasing Out Fossil Fuels
   - Renewable energy is now cheaper than coal (Lazard, 2023)
   - But 500,000 workers rely on fossil fuel jobs (BLS, 2023)
   Solution:
   - Green job guarantees in solar/wind sectors
   - Retraining programs modeled after GI Bill
   2. Decentralizing Energy
   - Microgrids (like Puerto Rico's post-Maria solar farms) prevent system-wide failures

Section 3: The Climate Resilience Corps

   Modeled After Historical Successes

    - CCC (1930s): Employed 3 million in conservation
    - AmeriCorps: Modern disaster response
    Tasks:
    - Reforestation to curb wildfires
    - Wetland restoration for flood control
    Section 4: Legal Safeguards Against Climate Displacement
    Preventing a New Dust Bowl
    - Rights for climate migrants (following UN guidelines)
    - Farmland conservation subsidies

Addressing Racism and Hate Speech in the Creation of a New U.S. Constitution: A Historical and Political Imperative

The United States Constitution, ratified in 1788, has long served as the bedrock of American governance. However, its enduring legacy is not without blemish. Historically, it was crafted in an era that tolerated slavery, excluded Indigenous peoples, and marginalized women and non-white citizens. While subsequent amendments have expanded civil rights and protections, systemic racism and hate speech remain persistent challenges in American society. As discussions surrounding constitutional reform gain traction—particularly in light of growing social divisions, political polarization, and calls for racial justice—it becomes imperative to consider how a new or revised U.S. Constitution could more effectively address racism and hate speech at their roots.

This article explores the historical context of racism in the original Constitution, analyzes the limitations of current legal frameworks in combating hate speech, and argues for the inclusion of explicit anti-racist provisions and hate speech protections in any future constitutional revision.

I. The Original Sin: Racism Embedded in the Founding Document

The U.S. Constitution, while celebrated as a beacon of liberty and democracy, was written by white male elites who lived in a society built on racial hierarchies. Several clauses implicitly or explicitly supported slavery and racial discrimination:

- The Three-Fifths Compromise (Article I, Section 2) counted enslaved Black individuals as three-fifths of a person for representation purposes, dehumanizing them while simultaneously increasing political power for slaveholding states.

- The Fugitive Slave Clause (Article IV, Section 2) protected the right of enslavers to recover escaped enslaved people, reinforcing the institution of slavery.

- The Commerce and Slave Trade Compromise (Article I, Section 9) delayed federal regulation of the transatlantic slave trade until 1808, entrenching the economic foundations of slavery (U.S. Constitution[cxvi], 1787).

These provisions reflect a foundational compromise with racism, prioritizing political unity over human dignity and equality (Blight[cxvii], 2009). While the post-Civil War Reconstruction Amendments—especially the Thirteenth, Fourteenth, and Fifteenth—sought to rectify these injustices, structural inequalities persisted through Jim Crow laws, redlining, mass incarceration, and other forms of institutional racism.

II. Current Legal Frameworks and Their Limitations

Today, the First Amendment protects freedom of speech, including hate speech, unless it incites imminent lawless action or constitutes true threats (Brandenburg v. Ohio[cxviii], 1969; Virginia v. Black[cxix], 2003). This high threshold leaves many forms of racist expression legally permissible, even when they contribute to societal harm, intimidation, and violence against minority communities.

In contrast, many democratic nations—including Germany, Canada, and members of the European Union—have adopted legal frameworks that balance free speech with protections against hate speech and incitement to hatred (European Commission[cxx], 2020; Canadian Human Rights Act[cxxi], 1975). These countries recognize that unchecked hate speech can erode democratic norms, fuel violence, and undermine social cohesion.

In the U.S., legal remedies for hate speech often fall under civil rights statutes such as Title VII of the Civil Rights Act of 1964 or hate crime legislation like the Matthew Shepard and James Byrd Jr. Hate Crimes Prevention Act[cxxii] (2009). However, these measures are reactive rather than preventive and lack the constitutional authority necessary to fully combat systemic racism and hate-based discourse.

III. A Constitutional Imperative: Embedding Anti-Racism and Hate Speech Protections

To address these shortcomings, a new or revised U.S. Constitution should include explicit language that:
1. Recognizes the inherent dignity and equality of all people, regardless of race, ethnicity, religion, gender, or national origin.
2. Prohibits state and federal governments from enacting policies or practices that perpetuate racial discrimination, building

upon the Equal Protection Clause of the Fourteenth Amendment.

3. Establishes a framework for regulating hate speech, particularly when it incites violence, promotes systemic discrimination, or undermines public safety and democratic participation.

Such provisions would align the Constitution with modern understandings of human rights and international standards, including those outlined in the International Convention on the Elimination of All Forms of Racial Discrimination (ICERD) and the International Covenant on Civil and Political Rights (ICCPR[cxxiii]), both of which the U.S. has ratified but implemented incompletely (United Nations[cxxiv], 1965, 1966).

Critics may argue that such changes would infringe upon First Amendment freedoms. However, constitutional design allows for balancing rights—just as freedom of religion does not permit human sacrifice, freedom of speech need not protect speech that directly threatens the rights and lives of others (Sunstein[cxxv], 1995).

IV. Toward a More Perfect Union: Lessons from Comparative Constitutionalism

Other nations have successfully integrated anti-racist and anti-hate speech principles into their constitutions. For example:

- Germany's Basic Law (Grundgesetz) explicitly prohibits anyone from "publicly or in a meeting approving, denying or trivializing an act committed under national socialism" (Article 21), reflecting a commitment to confronting historical injustice (Federal Republic of Germany[cxxvi], 1949).

- South Africa's Constitution, drafted after apartheid, includes strong anti-discrimination clauses and empowers the government to promote equality and prevent hate speech (Republic of South Africa[cxxvii], 1996).

These models demonstrate that constitutional democracies can uphold freedom of expression while also protecting vulnerable groups from harmful, dehumanizing rhetoric.

The time has come to confront the unfinished work of the American founding. A new U.S. Constitution—or a significant revision of the existing one—must reckon with the nation's legacy of racism and provide a robust legal foundation for addressing hate speech and systemic discrimination. By embedding anti-racist principles and redefining the boundaries of protected speech, the United States can fulfill its promise of liberty and justice for all.

Addressing the Constitutional Right to Unionize and the Abolition of Modern Labor Slavery

The struggle for workers' rights is deeply intertwined with the broader pursuit of human dignity and freedom. In the United States, the constitutional right to unionize and the persistent existence of modern forms of labor slavery represent two critical, yet often overlooked, fronts in this struggle. Addressing these issues is essential for the realization of true liberty and justice in the workplace.

The Constitutional Right to Unionize

The right to unionize is fundamentally protected by the U.S. Constitution. The First Amendment guarantees freedoms of speech, assembly, and petition, which courts have recognized as encompassing the freedom of association core element of unionization. This right allows individuals to collectively pursue their interests, including through union activity, and is further reinforced by the Due Process Clause of the Fourteenth Amendment, which assures liberty, including the right to organize for shared values (LaborLab, 2024)[cxxviii].

Federal law further enshrines these rights. The National Labor Relations Act (NLRA) of 1935 explicitly guarantees employees the right to organize, join unions, engage in collective bargaining, and take collective action for mutual aid and protection (National Labor Relations Board, n.d.) [cxxix]. Section 7 of the NLRA protects workers from employer retaliation when they engage in union activities, such as distributing literature, soliciting support, or discussing union matters with coworkers (LaborLab, 2024).

The Supreme Court has acknowledged the fundamental nature of these rights. In NLRB v. Jones & Laughlin Steel Corp., the Court recognized labor collective action as a "fundamental right," affirming that unions advance both commerce and constitutional values, including the "full freedom of association" (ACS, 2023)[cxxx].

The Persistence of Modern Labor Slavery

Despite the abolition of chattel slavery by the Thirteenth Amendment in 1865, which declared that "neither slavery nor involuntary servitude, except as a punishment for crime... shall exist within the United States," a significant loophole remains (National

Archives, 2022)[cxxxi]. This exception has allowed for the continuation of forced labor, particularly within the criminal justice system, where incarcerated individuals can be compelled to work, often under exploitative conditions (Vera Institute, 2024)[cxxxii].

Modern slavery extends beyond prison labor. It encompasses forced labor, debt bondage, human trafficking, and other forms of exploitation in which individuals cannot refuse or leave work due to threats, violence, coercion, or abuse of power (Walk Free, n.d.)[cxxxiii]. In many cases, workers endure degrading conditions, excessive hours, and psychological coercion, often under the guise of legitimate employment (SciELO, 2023)[cxxxiv].

Internationally, the right to unionize and protection from forced labor are recognized as fundamental human rights. Article 23 of the Universal Declaration of Human Rights and the International Labour Organization's conventions affirm these protections, yet enforcement remains inconsistent, and millions remain vulnerable to modern forms of slavery (LaborLab, 2024); (SciELO, 2023).

The Need for Reform

1. Strengthening Constitutional Protections for Unionization

- Ensuring that all workers, including those in marginalized or precarious sectors, can freely exercise their right to unionize is vital for advancing the workplace democracy and economic justice (LaborLab, 2024).

- Legislative and judicial reinforcement of these rights is necessary to counteract employer resistance and legal loopholes that undermine collective bargaining (ACS, 2023).

2. Abolishing Modern Labor Slavery

- The exception clause in the Thirteenth Amendment must be addressed through measures such as the proposed Abolition Amendment, which seeks to prohibit slavery and involuntary servitude in all circumstances, including as punishment for a crime (Vera Institute, 2024).

- Comprehensive enforcement of anti-slavery laws, alongside international cooperation, is essential to eradicate forced labor in all its forms (Walk Free, n.d.); (SciELO, 2023).

3. Upholding Human Dignity

- Both the right to unionize and the fight against modern slavery are rooted in the principle of human dignity. Workers must be empowered to advocate for fair wages, safe conditions, and respect, free from coercion or exploitation.

The constitutional right to unionize and the abolition of modern labor slavery are inseparable from the ideals of liberty and justice. Addressing these issues requires not only legislative and judicial action but also a societal commitment to upholding the dignity and rights of all workers.

Taxation and Financial Regulation of Religious Institutions in Secular Democracies

Taxing churches and subjecting them to AML regulations are not attacks on religious liberty but necessary steps to uphold the rule of law. By closing loopholes that enable financial crimes and ensuring equitable fiscal contributions, secular democracies can foster transparency while respecting diverse beliefs.

In secular democracies, the balance between religious freedom and public accountability remains a contentious issue. While churches have historically enjoyed tax exemptions and minimal financial oversight, modern challenges—including systemic financial abuse and money laundering—demand reforms to align religious institutions with broader societal obligations.

Historical Context of Tax Exemptions

The U.S. tax code exempts religious organizations from federal taxation under Section 501(c)(3), a practice rooted in the First Amendment's Establishment Clause. The Supreme Court upheld this exemption in Walz v. Tax Commission (1970), arguing that taxing churches would create excessive entanglement between state and religion[cxxxv]. However, critics contend that exemptions functionally subsidize religious activities, costing governments billions in lost revenue while enabling financial opacity.

The Case for Taxation

1. Equity and Fiscal Responsibility: Secular democracies prioritize equal treatment under the law. Tax exemptions for churches contrast sharply with the tax burdens shouldered by secular nonprofits and businesses. For instance, churches are not required to file Form 990, which mandates financial transparency for other tax-exempt entities[cxxxvi]. This disparity undermines fiscal fairness and public trust.
2. Preventing Exploitation: Tax exemptions have enabled abuse, such as embezzlement and lavish spending by religious leaders. A 2024 case study revealed a church administrator who stole $350,000 through unauthorized checks and credit card purchases, exploiting lax oversight[cxxxvii]. Taxing churches

would incentivize stricter financial accountability.

Modern Labor Slavery and Financial Crime Risks

1. Money Laundering Vulnerabilities: Religious institutions' financial opacity makes them susceptible to exploitation. For example, a 2020 investigation found Argentinian branches of a global church depositing millions in unexplained cash, highlighting how tithes and donations can mask illicit funds[cxxxviii]. Internal fraud costs U.S. churches approximately $63 million annually, with one leader laundering $1.4 million through religious channels[cxxxix].

2. Regulatory Gaps: Unlike banks, churches are not subject to anti-money laundering (AML) regulations. A 2023 FATF report noted that religious organizations in North Macedonia and Europe often lack mechanisms to detect or report suspicious transactions, urging reforms like mandatory financial disclosures and risk assessments[cxl].

Policy Recommendations

1. Taxation Reforms:
 - Revoke blanket tax exemptions, requiring churches to pay property and income taxes unless they meet strict charitable activity criteria.

- Mandate Form 990 filings to ensure transparency.

2. AML Compliance:
- Include churches in AML frameworks, requiring suspicious transaction reports and due diligence on large donations.
- Strengthen penalties for financial misconduct, as seen in cases of clergy embezzlement.

3. International Cooperation:
- Adopt recommendations from the FATF to harmonize oversight of religious nonprofits globally, particularly in regions where churches evade cross-border financial scrutiny.

Addressing Counterarguments

Proponents of exemptions argue that taxation infringes on religious freedom. However, secular democracies must distinguish between belief and institutional privilege. As the Supreme Court noted in Walz, exemptions are not constitutionally required but a legislative choice. Reforming this choice to curb abuse aligns with democratic values of accountability and equity.

Reforming Supreme Court Selection: A Case for Congressional Oversight and Fixed Terms

The U.S. Supreme Court's lifetime appointments and presidential nomination process have increasingly sparked debates about judicial accountability, politicization, and institutional legitimacy. Proposals for reform, including fixed terms and congressional selection mechanisms, aim to align the Court with modern democratic principles while preserving judicial independence.

Historical Foundations and Current Challenges

Under Article II of the U.S. Constitution, Supreme Court Justices[cxli] are nominated by the President and confirmed by the Senate, serving lifetime tenures "during good Behaviour" (U.S. Const. art. II, § 2)[cxlii],[cxliii] This system, designed to insulate justices from political pressures, has faced criticism for enabling prolonged ideological dominance and fostering contentious confirmation battles. Recent appointees, often elevated from federal appellate benches in their 30s or 40s, have been criticized for lacking diverse professional experiences, leading to perceptions of a Court disconnected from societal realities[cxliv].

The Senate's 2017 adoption of the "nuclear option"—lowering the cloture threshold to 51 votes for Supreme Court nominations—exacerbated partisan tensions, reducing confirmations to majority-party exercises[cxlv]. Lifetime tenure, meanwhile, has allowed justices to shape law for decades, as seen in rulings on abortion rights, presidential immunity, and voting rights[cxlvi][cxlvii].

Proposed Reforms: Five-Year Terms and Congressional Selection

A reconstituted constitutional framework could address these issues through two interconnected reforms:

1. Fixed Five-Year Terms:

Replacing lifetime appointments with staggered five-year terms would ensure regular turnover, preventing prolonged ideological stagnation. This aligns with proposals like the Supreme Court Term Limits and Regular Appointments Act (2021), which advocates 18-year terms to balance stability and refreshment[cxlviii]. Shorter terms, however, could enhance responsiveness to evolving societal norms while mitigating the stakes of individual appointments.

2. Congressional Selection Process:

Transferring nomination authority from the President to Congress would democratize judicial selection. Drawing from historical debates at the Constitutional Convention[cxlix], where delegates like James Madison favored legislative appointments to curb executive overreach[cl], a bicameral committee could vet candidates based on legal expertise, ethical standards, and professional diversity.

Addressing Counterarguments

Critics argue that fixed terms might incentivize justices to seek reappointment, politicizing decisions. To mitigate this, terms could be non-renewable, as proposed in state-level models where appellate judges serve set terms without reappointment[cli]. Congressional selection, while potentially partisan, could be structured with bipartisan oversight committees and transparency mandates, akin to ethics reforms urged by President Biden in 2024[clii].

Redesigning the Supreme Court selection through fixed terms and congressional oversight would restore public trust and align judiciary with contemporary democratic values. By prioritizing accountability without sacrificing independence, such reforms could ensure the Court remains a guardian of constitutional principles rather than a reflection of transient political winds.

Constitutional Regulation of Campaign Finance: Preventing the Incursion of Private Corporations and Foreign Governments in American Democracy

The integrity of democratic elections hinges on public trust that political power is derived from the will of the people—not the financial influence of private corporations or foreign entities. Yet, over the past several decades, U.S. political campaigns have become increasingly dominated by massive infusions of money from corporate interests, Super PACs, and, in some cases, illicit contributions from abroad. These trends threaten the foundational principle of representative democracy: one person, one vote.

While existing laws such as the Federal Election Campaign Act (FECA) of 1971 and the Bipartisan Campaign Reform Act (BCRA) of 2002 sought to regulate campaign finance, landmark Supreme Court decisions like Citizens United v. FEC (2010) have severely weakened these protections, allowing unprecedented levels of corporate spending in politics. Furthermore, concerns about foreign interference—most notably during the 2016 presidential election—have exposed vulnerabilities in the current system.

This article argues that the only durable solution to safeguard democratic legitimacy lies in a constitutional amendment mandating robust regulation of campaign finance, explicitly prohibiting unlimited corporate expenditures and ensuring transparency and accountability for all sources of political funding.

I. The Historical Evolution of Campaign Finance Law

Campaign finance regulation in the United States has long been shaped by tensions between free speech and electoral fairness. In 1907, the Tillman Act became the first federal law to prohibit corporations from contributing directly to political campaigns (U.S. Federal Election Commission[cliii] [FEC], n.d.). Over time, Congress expanded this framework with FECA, which established disclosure requirements and contribution limits. However, enforcement remained weak until the creation of the Federal Election Commission (FEC) in 1974 following the Watergate scandal.

Despite these reforms, loopholes persisted. The rise of "soft money" in the 1990s led to the passage of BCRA[cliv], also known as the McCain-Feingold Act, which aimed to close those gaps by banning unrestricted donations to political parties and regulating issue advocacy ads (Hasen[clv], 2016).

Yet, these legislative efforts were undercut by judicial rulings that prioritized corporate political expression over democratic integrity.

II. Judicial Erosion of Campaign Finance Protections

The most consequential turning point came in 2010 with the Supreme Court's decision in Citizens United v. Federal Election Commission, 558 U.S. 310. The Court ruled that restrictions on independent political expenditures by corporations and unions violated the First Amendment's protection of free speech. This opened the floodgates for Super PACs and other entities to spend unlimited sums on behalf of candidates, provided they did not coordinate directly with campaigns.

As a result, political spending skyrocketed. According to OpenSecrets[clvi] (2022), total outside spending in federal elections increased from $338 million in 2008 to over $1.4 billion in 2020, much of it funneled through dark money groups with opaque donor sources.

Moreover, the decision disproportionately empowered wealthy individuals and corporations, undermining the egalitarian ideal of equal political voice. As Justice Stevens warned in his dissent, "The

Court's ruling threatens to undermine the integrity of elected institutions across the Nation" (Citizens United v. FEC[clvii], 2010, Stevens, J., dissenting).

III. Foreign Interference and National Security Risks

Beyond domestic concerns, the lack of comprehensive campaign finance regulation has left U.S. elections vulnerable to foreign influence. While the Foreign Agents Registration Act (FARA) of 1938 and subsequent statutes technically prohibit foreign nationals from contributing to U.S. elections, enforcement has been inconsistent and reactive.

The 2016 election highlighted how digital platforms could be exploited to disseminate disinformation and manipulate voter sentiment without direct monetary transfers. Additionally, investigations revealed that Russian actors[clviii] used social media and intermediaries to interfere in the election, exploiting weaknesses in disclosure and oversight mechanisms (Mueller Report[clix], 2019).

More recently, reports have surfaced of foreign governments attempting to influence U.S. politicians through legal channels, including lobbying firms, think tanks, and campaign donations routed through shell companies (Vogel & Robles[clx], 2020). These practices underscore the urgent need for structural reform.

IV. A Constitutional Solution: Regulating Campaign Finance at Its Core

Given the limitations of statutory law and the judiciary's reluctance to uphold strong campaign finance regulations, the only viable path forward is a constitutional amendment that:

1. Clarifies that money is not equivalent to speech, reversing the precedent set in Citizens United.
2. Prohibits unlimited independent expenditures by corporations and unions, restoring the balance between economic and political power.
3. Mandates full transparency of all political contributions and expenditures, including those made through third-party organizations.
4. Bars any contributions or expenditures by foreign individuals, governments, or entities, with strict penalties for violations.
5. Empowers Congress and states to establish reasonable limits on campaign spending and contributions, promoting electoral equity.

Such an amendment would align the U.S. more closely with international democratic standards. Countries like Canada, Germany, and Australia impose strict limits on political advertising, require real-time disclosure of donors, and restrict corporate and union spending in elections (IDEA[clxi], 2021).

V. Conclusion: Restoring Democracy Through a new Constitution

The unchecked flow of money into U.S. politics poses a profound threat to the legitimacy of the democratic process. Without a constitutional foundation for campaign finance regulation, future efforts to curb corruption, ensure transparency, and protect against foreign interference will remain vulnerable to judicial reversal and partisan manipulation.

By adopting a new Constitution to reassert the primacy of democratic participation over financial influence, the United States can begin to restore public trust, strengthen electoral integrity, and reaffirm its commitment to self-governance in the truest sense.

"Democracy is a small, hard core of common agreement, surrounded by a rich variety of individual differences."
James B. Conant

Chapter 3: A Parliamentary Government

The Flaws of the Presidential System: A Case Study of U.S. President Number 47 and the Need for a Parliamentary Alternative

The American presidential system, established in 1789, has long been viewed as a model of democratic governance. However, its structural features—particularly the concentration of executive power, lack of accountability mechanisms, and insulation from legislative oversight—have increasingly revealed vulnerabilities that enable corruption, authoritarian tendencies, and cruelty.

This article argues that the unchecked powers inherent in the U.S. presidential system contributed to the rise and actions of individuals like DT[clxii], and proposes a transition to a parliamentary system as a means of preventing future democratic erosion through enhanced accountability, collective leadership, and institutional checks on executive authority.

I. The Concentration of Power: Structural Vulnerabilities in the Presidential System

In a presidential system, the head of state and head of government are fused into one role—the president—who wields significant unilateral power. Unlike parliamentary systems, where prime ministers must maintain the confidence of the legislature, U.S. presidents serve fixed terms regardless of performance or misconduct (Linz[clxiii], 1990).

This structure allowed president 47 to bypass congressional oversight, attack the free press, undermine judicial independence, and promote policies rooted in xenophobia and racial division without facing immediate political consequences. For instance, his administration's family separation policy at the southern border was implemented via executive directive, highlighting how the executive can act unilaterally without sufficient legislative restraint (Kerwin, Warren, & Warren[clxiv], 2018).

Moreover, impeachment a rare and politically charged process—proved insufficiently as a deterrent. Despite being impeached twice by the House of Representatives[clxv], this ex-president was acquitted both times in the Senate, underscoring the partisan nature of the impeachment mechanism and its limited effectiveness as an accountability tool (Binder[clxvi], 2021).

II. Corruption and Cruelty: The Case of President 45 as a Precedent

Although not yet labeled as such by all scholars, many analysts have documented how 45's presidency exhibited traits of autocratic behavior, including:

- Erosion of democratic norms: He attacked the legitimacy of elections, undermined public trust in institutions, and promoted conspiracy theories that culminated in the January 6 Capitol riot (Levitsky & Ziblatt[clxvii], 2018).

- Abuse of public resources: President 47 used his office for personal gain, violating the Emoluments Clause of the Constitution and leveraging his position to benefit his businesses (Dodge[clxviii], 2019).

- Dehumanizing rhetoric and policy: His administration enacted cruel immigration policies, demonized minorities, and normalized hate speech, contributing to a broader culture of intolerance (Benkler, Faris, & Roberts[clxix], 2018).

These patterns illustrate how a flawed system enabled a flawed leader to operate with minimal institutional constraint. In contrast, parliamentary democracies typically offer more frequent opportunities for no-confidence votes, cabinet oversight, and rapid removal of leaders who breach democratic norms (Cheibub[clxx], 2007).

III. The Parliamentary Alternative: Accountability, Flexibility, and Collective Leadership

A parliamentary system offers several advantages over the presidential model:
1. Collective Responsibility: In parliamentary systems, the executive branch is composed of a cabinet drawn from the legislature, ensuring greater collaboration and reducing the risk of one-person rule.
2. Enhanced Accountability: Prime ministers can be removed through votes of no confidence, allowing for swift responses to misconduct or loss of public support.
3. Reduced Polarization: Coalition-building and consensus politics are often necessary in parliamentary systems, fostering compromise and moderation (Lijphart[clxxi], 2012).

Countries like Canada, Germany, and the United Kingdom have demonstrated resilience against authoritarian drift precisely because their systems allow for continuous legislative scrutiny and shared governance. For example, in 2019, the UK Parliament played a central role in shaping Brexit policy despite a strong executive under Prime Minister Boris Johnson, illustrating the power of parliamentary oversight (Bogdanor[clxxii], 2020).

IV. Preventing Future Presidents Like 47: Constitutional Reform and Institutional Design

To prevent the rise of future leaders who might exploit the weaknesses of the presidential system, the U.S. could consider:
- Adopting a parliamentary model, where the executive is dependent on legislative confidence.
- Establishing a stronger ombudsman or ethics commission, independent of the executive, to monitor corruption and abuse of power.
- Reforming executive orders and emergency powers, limiting their scope and requiring legislative approval after a certain period.
- Strengthening campaign finance laws and media regulations to curb misinformation and oligarchic influence.

Such reforms would align the U.S. with global democratic trends and help insulate the country from the risks associated with unchecked executive authority.

The flaws of the American presidential system were laid bare during the tenure of President 47 and pose a continuing threat to democratic stability. The hypothetical specter of a future "President 47" should serve as a warning: without structural reform, the U.S. remains vulnerable to authoritarianism, corruption, and cruelty. Transitioning to a parliamentary system could restore balance, enhance accountability, and protect the nation from repeating its most dangerous political experiments.

The Case for Parliamentary Democracy: How a Coalition-Based System Could Stabilize American Governance

The presidential system's vulnerabilities—dementia risks, market manipulation, authoritarian drift—are structural. Transitioning to a parliamentary model would:

✓ *Distribute executive power*

✓ *Stabilize global markets*

✓ *Prevent unilateral disruptions*

The Constitution was meant to evolve. As Hamilton wrote in Federalist 1, "It seems to have been reserved to the people of this country... to decide whether societies are capable of establishing good government by

reflection and choice." That reflection now points to parliamentary reform.
A More Resilient Democracy

The Perils of Presidential Supremacy

The United States' presidential system, designed in the 18th century, has increasingly revealed dangerous flaws in the modern era. The concentration of power in a single executive—subject to cognitive decline, erratic behavior, or authoritarian impulses—poses systemic risks not just domestically, but globally. Recent examples include:

- Market volatility triggered by presidential rhetoric (e.g., tweets threatening trade wars or confusing policy statements) (Baker et al., 2020)

- Foreign policy instability due to abrupt reversals in diplomatic commitments (Allison, 2021)

- Erosion of democratic norms when presidents exploit executive powers to evade accountability (Levitsky & Ziblatt[clxxiii], 2018)

A parliamentary system, where executive authority derives from legislative coalitions rather than a singular presidency, could mitigate these risks while enhancing governance stability.

Section 1: How Presidentialism Fails

1. The "Lone Decider" Problem

The U.S. presidency grants near-monarchical powers in foreign policy, regulatory control, and national emergencies—with few checks once elected. Historical examples:
- Woodrow Wilson's incapacitation (1919-1921), where his stroke left the nation leaderless (Cooper, 2008)
- Trump's erratic diplomacy, which destabilized alliances (Sanger, 2020)
- Biden's cognitive lapses, raising concerns about decision-making capacity (Parker & Dawsey, 2024)

2. Market and Global Instability
- Research shows presidential speeches can swing stock indices by 2-3% (Wolfers & Zitzewitz[clxxiv], 2018)
- In parliamentary systems (e.g., Germany, Canada), leadership is collective, reducing volatility (Lijphart, 2012)

3. Polarization and Gridlock
- Presidential systems encourage zero-sum politics (Linz[clxxv], 1990)
- Parliamentary democracies force coalition-building, as seen in Nordic states' climate policies

Section 2: How a U.S. Parliamentary System Would Work

1. Prime Minister & Cabinet from Congress
- The majority party (or coalition) selects the executive, removable via no-confidence votes
- Prevents "imperial presidency" scenarios (Schlesinger, 1973)

2. Collective Decision-Making
- No single person controls nuclear codes—requires cabinet consensus
- Market-sensitive policies debated in legislature first, not announced via tweet

3. Faster Crisis Response
- Parliamentary systems change leaders swiftly (e.g., UK's Johnson-to-Truss-to-Sunak transitions)
- Avoids years of leadership decline (e.g., Reagan's later Alzheimer's years)

Section 3: Counterarguments & Rebuttals

"Presidentialism Provides Stability"
→ Rebuttal: Data shows parliamentary democracies have longer average governance durations (Cheibub et al.[clxxvi], 2020)

"Americans Prefer Direct Elections"
→ Rebuttal: Parliamentary systems (e.g., Australia) still hold popular votes for legislators

"Coalitions Are Messy"

→ Rebuttal: Multiparty governance reduces extremism (e.g., Germany's far-right containment)

The Author

Juan Ramon Rodulfo Moya, **Defined by Nature**: Inhabitant of Planet Earth, Human, Son of Eladio Rodulfo and Briceida Moya, Brother of Gabriela, Gustavo and Katiuska, Father of Gabriel and Sofia; **Defined by society**: Venezuelan Citizen (Limited Human Rights by default), Friend of many, enemy of few, Neighbor, Student/Teacher/Student, Worker/Supervisor/Manager/Leader/Worker, Husband of K/Ex-Husband of K/Husband of Y; **Defined by the U.S. Immigration Office**: Legal Alien; **Classroom studies**: Master's Degree in Human Resource Management, English, Mandarin Chinese; **Real-World Studies**: Human Behavior; **Home Studios**: SEO Webmaster, Graphic Design, Application and Website Development, Internet and Social Media Marketing, Video Production, YouTube Branding, Part 107 Commercial Drone Pilot, Import-Export, Affiliate Marketing, Cooking, Laundry, Home Cleaning; **Work experience**: Public-Private-Entrepreneurial Sectors; **Other definitions:** Bitcoin Evangelist, Human Rights, Peace and Love Advocate.

Publications:

Books:

Why Maslow? How to use his theory to stay in Power Forever (2018)
¿Por qué Maslow? Cómo usar su teoría para permanecer en el Poder por siempre (2018)
Asylum Seekers (2018)
En busca de Asilo (2018)
Manual for Gorillas: 9 Rules to be the "FER-PECT" dictator (2019)
Manual para Gorilas: 9 Reglas para ser el dictador "FER-PECTO" (2019)
Why you must Play the Lottery (2019)
Por qué debes jugar la Lotería (2021)
Para Español Oprima #2: Speaking Spanish in Times of Xenophobia (2019)
Cause of Death: IGNORANCE, Human Behavior in Times of PANIC (2019)
Politics explained for Millennials, GENs XYZ and future generations (2022)
Política explicada para Millennials, GENs xyz y futuras generaciones (2022)
Las cenizas del Ejército Libertador (2023)
Remain Silent: The only right we have. The legal Aliens (2023)
Fortune Cookie Coaching 88 Motivational Tips Made of Fortune Cookies, Vol I (2024)
Vicky Erotic Tales, Vol I (2024)
TikTok Heroes in my Algorithm (2025)

AI at Home, transforming your child's Learning Experience (2025)
IA en Casa, Reinventando el aprendizaje de l@s niñ@s (2025)

Blogs:

Noticias de Nueva Esparta, Ubuntu Café, Coffee Secrets, Guaripete Pro, Rodulfox, Red Wasp Drone, Barista Pro, Gorila Travel, Fortune Cookie Coach, All Books, Vicky Toys.

Audiovisual Productions:

Podcasts:

Ubuntu Cafe | Vicky Erotic Tales | Fortune Cookie Coach | All Books, available at: juanrodulfo.com/podcasts

Music:

Albums: Margarita | Race to Extinction | Relaxed Panda | Amazonia | Cassiopeia | Caracas | Arcoiris Musical | Close Your Eyes, available at: juanrodulfo.com/music

Photography & Video:

On sale at Adobe Stock, iStock, Shutterstock, and Veectezy, available at: juanrodulfo.com/gallery

Social Media Profiles:

BlueSky / Twitter / FB / Instagram / TikTok/ VK / LinkedIn / Sina Weibo: @rodulfox

Google Author: https://g.co/kgs/grjtN5
Google Artist: https://g.co/kgs/H7Fiqg
Twitter: https://twitter.com/rodulfox
Facebook: https://facebook.com/rodulfox
LinkedIn: https://www.linkedin.com/in/rodulfox
Instagram: https://www.instagram.com/rodulfox/
VK: https://vk.com/rodulfox
TikTok: https://www.tiktok.com/@rodulfox
Trading View: https://www.tradingview.com/u/rodulfox/

Table of Contents

Introduction 5

Chapter 1: Referendum 11

Modernizing Democracy: The Case for a Next-Generation Blockchain Voting Platform 11

    Section 1: Why Current Voting Systems Fail 12

    Section 2: The Blockchain Voting Solution 13

    Section 3: Addressing Concerns ... 13

The Enduring Allure and Treacherous Path of the People's Vote: A Historian's Look at the Referendum 14

The American Referendum: A Tale of Two Democracies – Federal Abstinence, State Experimentation 19

The hypothetical questions: 25

    Chapter 2: a new Constitution 29

The Imperative of Embedding Fundamental Human Rights in a New U.S. Constitution 29

    Historical Context: The Bill of Rights and Its Evolution 30

    The Need for Explicit Human Rights Protections 30

    Recommendations for a New Constitution 31

Constitutionalizing Fundamental Rights: A Framework for Addressing America's Greatest Challenges 34
        The Case for Constitutionalizing Economic and Social Rights....................35
        Why Constitutionalizing is Necessary...38

Reimagining Immigration as an Engine of American Prosperity: A Case for Reform.......39
        Key reforms should include: 39
        Section 1: Immigrants Strengthen the U.S. Economy 40
        Section 2: The Case for a 5-Year Pathway to Citizenship 41
        Section 3: Work Visas with Voting Rights—A Democratic Imperative 41
        Section 4: Upgrading Immigration from Policing to Workforce Development 42
        Counterarguments & Rebuttals ...42

Ending America's Gun Violence Pandemic: A Policy Framework for Radical Reform 43
        1. Banning War Weapons in Civilian Hands..44
        2. Disarming Routine Policing.....45
        3. Psychological & Criminal Screening for Gun Owners 45

4. A National Firearm Registry 46
Counterarguments & Rebuttals ...46
Restoring Moral Values in Governance and Society: A Blueprint for Ethical Reform 47
Section 1: Replacing Political Oaths with Enforceable Contracts 48
Section 2: Elevating Teachers as Moral Architects 48
Section 3: Protecting Families to Strengthen Societal Values 49
Counterarguments & Rebuttals ...50
Direct Demographic Representation in a U.S. Congress with no Senate 50
The American Ideal of Representation: A Contested History 51
Design for Demographic Parity: The Mechanics of a Hypothetical System 52
Potential Advantages: The Allure of a Reflective Legislature 54
Profound Challenges and Criticisms 55
Historical and Comparative Insights 57
A Radical Vision with Deep Dilemmas 58
Toward a More Representative Democracy ...59
The Case for Eliminating the Electoral College and Gerrymandering in U.S. Elections 60

The Imperative of Church State Separation: Reexamining Religious Symbols in Government Functions 63
Historical and Constitutional Foundations....64
Key Issues Undermining Church State Separation...65
Why Strict Separation Matters.......................66
    Reforms for a Religiously Neutral Government..67
The Crisis of Purpose in American Education68
    Section 1: Why Education Must Become a Constitutional Right................69
    Section 2: The Citizen-First Curriculum Model 70
    Section 3: Implementation Framework.. 71
Climate Readiness: A Historical Imperative for National Survival 72
    Section 1: Climate Change as a Threat Multiplier 73
    Section 2: A Just Transition to Renewable Energy 74
    Section 3: The Climate Resilience Corps...74
Addressing Racism and Hate Speech in the Creation of a New U.S. Constitution: A Historical and Political Imperative 75
    I. The Original Sin: Racism Embedded in the Founding Document...76

II. Current Legal Frameworks and Their Limitations 77

III. A Constitutional Imperative: Embedding Anti-Racism and Hate Speech Protections 78

IV. Toward a More Perfect Union: Lessons from Comparative Constitutionalism 80

Addressing the Constitutional Right to Unionize and the Abolition of Modern Labor Slavery ... 81

The Constitutional Right to Unionize 81

The Persistence of Modern Labor Slavery 82

The Need for Reform 83

Taxation and Financial Regulation of Religious Institutions in Secular Democracies 85

The Case for Taxation 86

Modern Labor Slavery and Financial Crime Risks 87

Policy Recommendations 87

Addressing Counterarguments ... 88

Reforming Supreme Court Selection: A Case for Congressional Oversight and Fixed Terms 89

Historical Foundations and Current Challenges 89

    Proposed Reforms: Five-Year Terms and Congressional Selection 90

    Addressing Counterarguments 91

Constitutional Regulation of Campaign Finance: Preventing the Incursion of Private Corporations and Foreign Governments in American Democracy..92

    I. The Historical Evolution of Campaign Finance Law 93

    II. Judicial Erosion of Campaign Finance Protections................................94

    III. Foreign Interference and National Security Risks 95

    IV. A Constitutional Solution: Regulating Campaign Finance at Its Core 96

    V. Conclusion: Restoring Democracy Through a new Constitution 97

    Chapter 3: A Parliamentary Government 101

The Flaws of the Presidential System: A Case Study of U.S. President Number 47 and the Need for a Parliamentary Alternative........... 101

    I. The Concentration of Power: Structural Vulnerabilities in the Presidential System 102

    II. Corruption and Cruelty: The Case of President 45 as a Precedent 103

III. The Parliamentary Alternative: Accountability, Flexibility, and Collective Leadership 104

IV. Preventing Future Presidents Like 47: Constitutional Reform and Institutional Design 105

The Case for Parliamentary Democracy: How a Coalition-Based System Could Stabilize American Governance...................................106

The Perils of Presidential Supremacy 107

Section 1: How Presidentialism Fails 108

Section 2: How a U.S. Parliamentary System Would Work............................. 109

Section 3: Counterarguments & Rebuttals...109

The Author 113

Publications: 114

Books: 114

Blogs: 114

Audiovisual Productions:............................115

Podcasts: 115

Music: 115

Photography & Video: 116

Social Media Profiles: 116

Endnotes 125

Endnotes

[i] I agree with George Carlin of his statement that in this country there are not such thing as "rights" but "privileges", since they can be taken and or violated by demand by government itself.

[ii] Brennan Center for Justice. (2023). The state of voting machines in America.

[iii] U.S. Election Assistance Commission. (2023). Barriers to voter accessibility.

[iv] Nakamoto, S. (2008). Bitcoin: A peer-to-peer electronic cash system.

[v] Estonian Government. (2023). E-voting in Estonia: Security and transparency.

[vi] MIT Digital Currency Initiative. (2022). Blockchain voting: Risks and opportunities.

[vii] Gallagher, M., & Uleri, P. V. (Eds.). (1996). The referendum experience in Europe. Palgrave Macmillan.

[viii] Finley, M. I. (1983). Politics in the ancient world. Cambridge University Press.

[ix] Rousseau, J.-J. (1997). The social contract and other later political writings (V. Gourevitch, Ed. & Trans.). Cambridge University Press. (Original work published 1762), available at: https://www.ebsco.com/research-starters/literature-and-writing/social-contract-jean-jacques-rousseau

[x] Pateman, C. (2003). The idea of popular sovereignty: From Rousseau to modernity. Cambridge University Press.

[xi] Kobach, K. W. (1993). The referendum: Direct democracy in Switzerland. Dartmouth Publishing.

[xii] Butler, D., & Ranney, A. (Eds.). (1994). Referendums around the world: The growing use of direct democracy. American Enterprise Institute. Available at: https://www.ch.ch/en/votes-and-elections/referendum/:~:text=Amendments%20to%20t

he%20Constitution%20require,in%20the%20cantons%20and%20communes.

[xiii] Suksi, M. (1993). Bringing in the people: A comparison of constitutional forms and practices of the referendum. Martinus Nijhoff Publishers.

[xiv] Blocker, J. S. (2006). Alcohol, reform and society: The liquor issue in social context. Greenwood Press.

[xv] Qvortrup, M. (2005). A comparative study of referendums: Government by the people (2nd ed.). Manchester University Press.

[xvi] Barber, B. R. (1984). Strong democracy: Participatory politics for a new age. University of California Press.

[xvii] Fishkin, J. S. (2011). When the people speak: Deliberative democracy and public consultation. Oxford University Press.

[xviii] Brooks Eleanor, Civil Liberties Union for Europe (Liberties). (2023). Different Types of Democracy and Their Main Characteristics. Available at: https://www.liberties.eu/en/stories/types-of-democracy/44801

[xix] European Parliament Think Tank. (2022). Referendums on EU issues: Fostering civic engagement, Available at: https://www.europarl.europa.eu/thinktank/en/document/EPRS_IDA(2022)729358

[xx] Sartori, G. (1987). The theory of democracy revisited. Chatham House Publishers. Available at: https://journals.openedition.org/revus/7744:~:text=I%20consider%20here%20what%20I,options%20in%20ways%20that%20sometimes

[xxi] Madison, J. (1961). Federalist No. 10. In J. E. Cooke (Ed.), The Federalist (pp. 56-65). Wesleyan University Press. (Original work published 1787)

[xxii] LeDuc, L. (2003). The politics of direct democracy: Referendums in global perspective. Broadview Press. Available at:

https://www.birmingham.ac.uk/research/perspective/referendums

[xxiii] Sunstein, C. R. (2018). Republic: Divided democracy in the age of social media. Princeton University Press.

[xxiv] Bogdanor, V. (1981). The people and the party system: The referendum and electoral reform in British politics. Cambridge University Press.

[xxv] Tierney, S. (2012). Constitutional referendums: The theory and practice of republican deliberation. Oxford University Press.

[xxvi] Glencross, A. (2018). Why the UK Voted for Brexit: David Cameron's Great Miscalculation. Palgrave Macmillan.

[xxvii] Clarke, H. D., Goodwin, M., & Whiteley, P. (2017). Brexit: Why Britain voted to leave the European Union. Cambridge University Press.

[xxviii] Morel, L., & Qvortrup, M. (Eds.). (2018). The Routledge handbook to referendums and direct democracy. Routledge.

[xxix] Hamilton, L. (2022). The People's Will: Referendums and the Modern Democratic Crisis. Oxford University Press.

[xxx] Madison, J. (1961). Federalist No. 10. In J. E. Cooke (Ed.), The Federalist (pp. 56-65). Wesleyan University Press. (Original work published 1787)

[xxxi] Magleby, D. B. (1984). Direct legislation: Voting on ballot propositions in the United States. Johns Hopkins University Press.

[xxxii] Hofstadter, R. (1955). The age of reform: From Bryan to F.D.R. Alfred A. Knopf.

[xxxiii] Cronin, T. E. (1989). Direct democracy: The politics of initiative, referendum, and recall. Harvard University Press.

[xxxiv] Smith, D. A., & Tolbert, C. J. (2004). Educated by initiative: The effects of direct democracy on citizens and political organizations in the American states. University of Michigan Press.

[xxxv] Sears, D. O., & Citrin, J. (1985). Tax revolt: Something for nothing in California (Enlarged ed.). Harvard University Press.

[xxxvi] Obergefell v. Hodges, 576 U.S. 644 (2015).

[xxxvii] Ellis, R. J. (2012). The Development of the American Presidency (2nd ed.). Routledge.

[xxxviii] Bowler, S., & Donovan, T. (2000). Demanding choices: Opinion, voting, and direct democracy. University of Michigan Press.

[xxxix] Broder, D. S. (2000). Democracy derailed: Initiative campaigns and the power of money. Harcourt.

[xl] Gamble, B. S. (1997). Putting civil rights to a popular vote. American Journal of Political Science, 41(1), 245–269.

[xli] Persily, N., & Anderson, M. (2005). Regulating the initiative and referendum process. In N. Persily & J. F. Zimmerman (Eds.), The future of the California initiative process (pp. 1-28). University of California Press.

[xlii] USHistory.org. (n.d.). Bill of Rights and later amendments to the United States Constitution. https://www.ushistory.org/documents/amendments.htm

[xliii] National Archives. (2024, March 6). 14th Amendment to the U.S. Constitution: Civil Rights (1868). https://www.archives.gov/milestone-documents/14th-amendment

[xliv] ACLU of Northern California. (2023, December 11). Human rights and the US Constitution. https://www.aclunc.org/blog/human-rights-and-us-constitution

[xlv] Wikipedia. (2002, February 9). United States Bill of Rights. https://en.wikipedia.org/wiki/United_States_Bill_of_Rights

[xlvi] https://www.archives.gov/founding-docs/bill-of-rights/what-does-it-say

xlvii https://www.archives.gov/milestone-documents/14th-amendment

xlviii https://www.aclunc.org/blog/human-rights-and-us-constitution

xlix Pew Research Center. (2024). Top problems facing the U.S. Available at: https://www.pewresearch.org/politics/2024/05/23/top-problems-facing-the-u-s/

l KFF. (2023). Key facts about the uninsured population.

li WHO. (2020). Global health expenditure database.

lii Federal Reserve. (2023). Report on the economic well-being of U.S. households.

liii Stanford Basic Income Lab. (2021). UBI pilot findings.

liv Economic Policy Institute (EPI). (2023). The productivity-pay gap.

lv OECD. (2022). Minimum wage systems.

lvi Center for Reproductive Rights. (2023). Constitutional abortion rights worldwide.

lvii UN Resolution 64/292. (2010). The human right to water and sanitation.

lviii New American Economy. (2022). Immigrants' GDP contributions.

lix Pew Research Center. (2023). Projected U.S. labor shortages.

lx National Academies of Sciences. (2022). The integration of immigrants into American society.

lxi American Immigration Council. (2023). Immigrants' economic power.

lxii Cato Institute. (2023). The fiscal cost of ICE deportations.

lxiii Raskin, J. (2023). The history of non-citizen voting in America. Yale Law Journal, 132(4).

lxiv Centers for Disease Control and Prevention (CDC). (2022). Firearm mortality by state.

[lxv] Federal Bureau of Investigation (FBI). (2023). Active shooter incidents report.
[lxvi] Webster, D. W., et al. (2014). Evidence that the 1994 assault weapons ban reduced mass shootings. Journal of Urban Health, 91(5), 1-12.
[lxvii] Harvard Injury Control Research Center. (2016). Australia's gun buyback effects.
[lxviii] NYPD. (2018). Mass shooter warning signs study.
[lxix] Everytown Research. (2022). Guns and domestic violence.
[lxx] RAND Corporation. (2020). The effects of red flag laws.
[lxxi] U.S. Department of Justice (DOJ). (2023). Public integrity convictions.
[lxxii] Economic Policy Institute (EPI). (2023). Teacher pay penalty report.
[lxxiii] OECD. (2022). Education at a glance.
[lxxiv] World Health Organization (WHO). (2023). Global breastfeeding scorecard.
[lxxv] Pitkin, H. F. (1967). The concept of representation. University of California Press.
[lxxvi] Madison, J., Hamilton, A., & Jay, J. (1961). The Federalist Papers (C. Rossiter, Ed.). New American Library. (Original work published 1788)
[lxxvii] Keyssar, A. (2000). The right to vote: The contested history of democracy in the United States. Basic Books.
[lxxviii] Davidson, C., & Grofman, B. (Eds.). (1994). Quiet revolution in the South: The impact of the Voting Rights Act, 1965-1990. Princeton University Press.
[lxxix] Mansbridge, J. (1999). Should blacks represent blacks and women represent women? A contingent "yes." Journal of Politics, 61(3), 628–657.
[lxxx] Regents of the University of California v. Bakke, 438 U.S. 265 (1978).
[lxxxi] Appiah, K. A. (2018). The lies that bind: Rethinking identity. Liveright Publishing.

[lxxxii] Krook, M. L. (2009). Quotas for women in politics: Gender and candidate selection reform worldwide. Oxford University Press.

[lxxxiii] Lijphart, A. (1977). Democracy in plural societies: A comparative exploration. Yale University Press.

[lxxxiv] Guinier, L. (1994). The tyranny of the majority: Fundamental fairness in representative democracy. Free Press.

[lxxxv] Edwards, G. C. (2019). Why the Electoral College is Bad for America (3rd ed.). Yale University Press.

[lxxxvi] National Archives. (2021). Electoral College results. https://www.archives.gov/electoralcollege

[lxxxvii] Bugh, G. (2016). Electoral College Reform: Challenges and Possibilities. Routledge.

Brennan Center for Justice. (2022). Gerrymandering and the Voting Rights Act. https://www.brennancenter.org

[lxxxviii] Koza, J. R., Fadem, B., Grueskin, M., et al. (2013). Every Vote Equal: A State Based Plan for Electing the President by National Popular Vote. National Popular Vote Press.

[lxxxix] McGann, A. J., Smith, C. A., & Latner, M. (2016). Gerrymandering in America: The House of Representatives, the Supreme Court, and the Future of Popular Sovereignty. Cambridge University Press.

[xc] Wang, S. S.H. (2016). "Three tests for practical evaluation of partisan gerrymandering." Stanford Law Review, 68(6), 12631321.

[xci] Li, M., & Grofman, B. (2020). "The efficiency gap, voter turnout, and the competitiveness of U.S. House elections." Political Analysis, 28(2), 257270.

[xcii] Drutman, L. (2020). Breaking the Two Party Doom Loop: The Case for Multiparty Democracy in America. Oxford University Press.

[xciii] Cirincione, C., & Darling, T. A. (2019). "Assessing the impact of redistricting commissions." Election Law Journal, 18(3), 235250.

[xciv] Stephanopoulos, N., & McGhee, E. (2015). "Partisan gerrymandering and the efficiency gap." University of Chicago Law Review, 82(2), 831900.

[xcv] Cornell Law School. (n.d.). First Amendment. Legal Information Institute. https://www.law.cornell.edu/constitution/first_amendment

[xcvi] Jefferson, T. (1802). Letter to the Danbury Baptists. Library of Congress.

[xcvii] Green, S. K. (2015). Inventing a Christian America: The myth of the religious founding. Oxford University Press.

[xcviii] Aronow v. United States, 432 F.2d 242 (9th Cir. 1970).

[xcix] American Humanist Association v. United States, 2016 WL 3166223 (9th Cir. 2016).

[c] Kramnick, I., & Moore, R. L. (2005). The Godless Constitution: A moral defense of the secular state. W.W. Norton.

[ci] Lambert, F. (2003). The founding fathers and the place of religion in America. Princeton University Press.

[cii] Seidel, A. (2019). Fighting God: The atheist handbook for religious resistance. Sterling.

[ciii] Laycock, D. (2020). Religious liberty and the culture wars. Cambridge University Press.

[civ] Pew Research Center. (2022). America's changing religious landscape. https://www.pewresearch.org

[cv] Bhargava, R. (2013). Secularism and its critics. Oxford University Press.

[cvi] National Assessment of Educational Progress. (2022). Civics assessment report card. U.S. Department of Education.

[cvii] Business Roundtable. (2023). Workforce readiness survey. Washington, DC.

[cviii] OECD. (2023). Education at a glance 2023: OECD indicators. OECD Publishing.

[cix] Lipman, M. (2003). Thinking in education (2nd ed.). Cambridge University Press.

[cx] Stanford History Education Group. (2021). Civic online reasoning curriculum. Stanford University.

[cxi] Levine, P. (2022). Educating for democracy: Costs and benefits. Tufts University Press.

[cxii] World Economic Forum. (2023). Future of jobs report 2023. Geneva, Switzerland.

[cxiii] Diamond, J. (2005). Collapse: How societies choose to fail or succeed. Viking.

[cxiv] NOAA. (2023). Billion-dollar weather disasters.

[cxv] Pentagon. (2023). Climate risk analysis report.

[cxvi] U.S. Constitution. (1787). Article I, Sections 2 and 9; Article IV, Section 2.

[cxvii] Blight, D. W. (2009). Race and Reunion: The Civil War in American Memory. Harvard University Press.

[cxviii] Brandenburg v. Ohio, 395 U.S. 444 (1969).

[cxix] Virginia v. Black, 538 U.S. 343 (2003).

[cxx] Council of the European Union. (2020). EU Framework Decision on Combating Racism and Xenophobia. Retrieved from https://www.consilium.europa.eu/en/policies/fight-against-racism-xenophobia/

[cxxi] Canadian Human Rights Act, R.S.C. 1985, c. H-6.

[cxxii] Matthew Shepard and James Byrd Jr. Hate Crimes Prevention Act, Pub. L. No. 111-84, 123 Stat. 2190 (2009).

[cxxiii] United Nations. (1966). International Covenant on Civil and Political Rights (ICCPR). United Nations Treaty Series, 999, 171.

[cxxiv] United Nations. (1965). International Convention on the Elimination of All Forms of Racial Discrimination (ICERD). United Nations Treaty Series, 660, 195.

[cxxv] Sunstein, C. R. (1995). Free Markets and Social Justice. Oxford University Press.

[cxxvi] Federal Republic of Germany. (1949). Basic Law for the Federal Republic of Germany. Article 21.

[cxxvii] Republic of South Africa. (1996). Constitution of the Republic of South Africa. Chapter 9.

[cxxviii] LaborLab. (2024). The right to unionize. Available at: https://laborlab.us/resource/the_right_to_unionize/

[cxxix] National Labor Relations Board. (n.d.). National Labor Relations Act. https://www.nlrb.gov/guidance/key-reference-materials/national-labor-relations-act

[cxxx] ACS. (2023). The lost constitutional stakes of labor unions. https://www.acslaw.org/expertforum/the-lost-constitutional-stakes-of-labor-union

[cxxxi] National Archives. (2022). 13th Amendment to the U.S. Constitution: Abolition of Slavery (1865). https://www.archives.gov/milestone-documents/13th-amendment

[cxxxii] Vera Institute. (2024). Slavery is still legal for two million people in the U.S. https://www.vera.org/news/slavery-is-still-legal-for-two-million-people-in-the-u-s

[cxxxiii] Walk Free. (n.d.). What is modern slavery? https://www.walkfree.org/what-is-modern-slavery

[cxxxiv] SciELO. (2023). The modern slavery wheel as the new theoretical framework. https://www.scielo.br/j/cebape/a/LpKXnjqyQgjcnjyhjSBcpVx

[cxxxv] Britannica. (2025). Churches and taxes debate. https://www.britannica.com/procon/churches-and-taxes-debate

cxxxvi Ministry Brands. (2024). Church financial management: Principles and best practices. https://www.ministrybrands.com/church/management/financial

cxxxvii Church Law & Tax. (2024). Embezzling church funds: A case study. https://www.churchlawandtax.com/manage-finances/internal-controls/embezzling-church-funds-a-case-study

cxxxviii OCCRP. (2020). Holy rollers: The religious leaders using churches to launder illicit cash across the Americas. https://www.occrp.org/en/investigation/holy-rollers-the-religious-leaders-using-churches-to-launder-illicit-cash-across-the-americas

cxxxix Financial Crime Academy. (2025). Bank and church money laundering: Ecclesiastical crime. https://financialcrimeacademy.org/bank-and-church-money-laundering-ecclesiastical-crime

cxl Konekt. (n.d.). Comparative analysis and recommendations on religious NPOs. FATF Platform. https://fatfplatform.org/assets/Konekt_Comparative-Analyses-on-religious-NPOs.pdf

cxli IAALS. (2024). Term limits for the United States Supreme Court. https://iaals.du.edu/blog/updated-term-limits-united-states-supreme-court

cxlii Georgetown Law Library. (2015). Nomination & confirmation process. https://guides.ll.georgetown.edu/c.php?g=365722&p=2471070

cxliii U.S. Courts. (n.d.). Nomination process. https://www.uscourts.gov/about-federal-courts/educational-resources/supreme-court-landmarks/nomination-process

cxliv Bloomberg Law. (2023). Judicial nomination process leads to a Supreme Court of nobodies. https://news.bloomberglaw.com/us-law-week/judicial-nomination-process-leads-to-a-supreme-court-of-nobodies

cxlv https://guides.ll.georgetown.edu/c.php?g=365722&p=2471070

cxlvi https://bidenwhitehouse.archives.gov/briefing-room/statements-releases/2024/07/29/fact-sheet-president-biden-announces-bold-plan-to-reform-the-supreme-court-and-ensure-no-president-is-above-the-law/

cxlvii https://www.scotusblog.com/2024/07/biden-proposes-supreme-court-reforms/

cxlviiicxlvii Congress.gov. (2021). Supreme Court Term Limits and Regular Appointments Act of 2021. https://www.congress.gov/bill/117th-congress/house-bill/5140

cxlix Wikipedia. (2005). Convention to propose amendments to the United States Constitution. https://en.wikipedia.org/wiki/Convention_to_propose_amendments_to_the_United_States_Constitution

cl https://www.fjc.gov/history/talking/teaching-and-civic-outreach-resources-constitutional-origins-federal-judiciary-3

cli https://jcjl.pubpub.org/pub/state-statutory-qualifications-for-judges

clii The White House. (2024). President Biden announces bold plan to reform the Supreme Court. https://bidenwhitehouse.archives.gov/briefing-room/statements-releases/2024/07/29/fact-sheet-president-biden-announces-bold-plan-to-reform-the-supreme-court-and-ensure-no-president-is-above-the-law

cliii Federal Election Commission (FEC). (n.d.). History of Campaign Finance Law. https://www.fec.gov/help-candidates-and-committees/

cliv Brennan Center for Justice. (2021). Citizens United and the Rise of Dark Money. https://www.brennancenter.org

clv Hasen, R. L. (2016). Plutocrats United: Campaign Money, the Supreme Court, and the Distortion of American Elections. Yale University Press.

clvi OpenSecrets. (2022). Outside Spending. https://www.opensecrets.org

clvii Citizens United v. Federal Election Commission, 558 U.S. 310 (2010).

clviii U.S. Department of Justice. (2019). Report of the Special Counsel on Russian Interference in the 2016 Presidential Election.

clix Mueller, R. S. (2019). Report on the Investigation into Russian Interference in the 2016 Presidential Election. U.S. Department of Justice.

clx Vogel, K. P., & Robles, F. (2020, February 17). How Foreign Powers Secretly Influence U.S. Politics. The New York Times. https://www.nytimes.com

clxi IDEA (International Institute for Democracy and Electoral Assistance). (2021). Global State of Electoral Integrity: Campaign Finance Regulations. https://www.idea.int

clxii Donald Trump

clxiii Linz, J. J. (1990). The Perils of Presidentialism. Journal of Democracy, 1(1), 51–69. https://doi.org/10.1353/jod.1990.0006

clxiv Kerwin, D., Warren, R., & Warren, W. (2018). The End of Asylum: Replacing the Global System of Protection with Hostility, Detention, and Deportation. Praeger.

clxv United States Congress. (2021). Report Pursuant to Section 2(a)(9) of the Congressional Accountability Act of 1995 Regarding Former President Donald J. Trump. U.S. House of Representatives.

clxvi Binder, S. A. (2021). The Impeachment of Donald Trump: Partisan Conflict and the Politics of Presidential Removal. Brookings Institution Press.

clxvii Levitsky, S., & Ziblatt, D. (2018). How Democracies Die. Crown.

clxviii Dodge, W. S. (2019). International Comity in Comparative Perspective. Cambridge University Press.

clxix Benkler, Y., Faris, R., & Roberts, H. (2018). Network Propaganda: Manipulation, Disinformation, and Radicalization in American Politics. Oxford University Press.

clxx Cheibub, J. A. (2007). Presidentialism, Parliamentarism, and Democracy. Cambridge University Press.

clxxi Lijphart, A. (2012). Patterns of Democracy: Government Forms and Performance in Thirty-Six Countries. Yale University Press.

clxxii Bogdanor, V. (2020). The New British Constitution. Hart Publishing.

clxxiii Levitsky, S., & Ziblatt, D. (2018). How democracies die. Crown.

clxxiv Wolfers, J., & Zitzewitz, E. (2018). How presidential rhetoric moves markets. NBER Working Paper.

clxxv Linz, J. J. (1990). The perils of presidentialism. Journal of Democracy, 1(1), 51-69.

clxxvi Cheibub, J. A., et al. (2020). Democracy and dictatorship revisited. Public Choice, 183(1), 1-35.

www.ingramcontent.com/pod-product-compliance
Lightning Source LLC
LaVergne TN
LVHW052245070526
838201LV00113B/347/J